BPTC Revision: Prepare to Pass
Civil Litigation, Evidence and Remedies
2014-2015

BPTC Revision: Prepare to Pass
Civil Litigation, Evidence and Remedies
2014-2015

Gillian Woodworth

Upfish Business Services Ltd

2014

First Printing: 2014

ISBN: 978-1-291-80337-2

Upfish Business Services Ltd
153 Park Street Lane
St Albans
AL2 2AZ

Ordering Information:
Special discounts are available on quantity purchases by corporations, associations, educators, and others. For details, contact the publisher at the above listed address or at gwoodworth.upfish.law@gmail.com

CONTENTS

Appendices

OVERTURE

This book provides specific guidance on preparing for the centrally set BPTC assessment in Civil Litigation, Evidence and Remedies. In addition to setting out the knowledge required for the BPTC assessment there are worked examples of the CPR in action, as well as diagrams and flow charts to help you cement your learning and understanding. This book aims to help you to acquire the necessary skills to apply your knowledge in the way necessary to pass the assessment.

It deals with every element of the required content in the syllabus for the BPTC assessment as set by the Bar Standards Board. This book cross-references the syllabus, the White Book and the Civil Litigation, Evidence and Remedies process so that you can be confident that you have encountered all of the requirements set by the Board.

Properly used, this book should ensure that you clearly understand Civil Litigation, Evidence and Remedies by the time you are examined on it. It provides opportunities to promote your learning through active engagement with the White Book and includes appendices with useful ideas for study methods, for exam preparation and for approaching the Multiple Choice and Short Answer Questions in the actual assessment.

This book follows the civil litigation process in a logical order from pre-action through to trial and beyond. It gives an overview of Civil Litigation, Evidence and Remedies, helpful to all students and practitioners whose vocation is the legal profession.

> *You are __strongly__ recommended to become conversant with the contents of the appendices of this book before beginning to work your way through the substantive chapters.*

The author, Gillian Woodworth, transferred from full-time professional practice to working in full-time legal education in 1995. Since then she has spent nearly 20 years training students on both academic and professional legal courses and as a regulator of those courses. She worked for 10 years at BPP as a tutor, course director and Director of Staff Training and Development; she has worked as a visiting lecturer at what is now the University of Law; she then worked in the Education and Training department of the Solicitors Regulation Authority prior to moving to The City Law School, City University.

Gillian worked for over 6 years full-time at City, teaching and assessing initially on the on the Bar Vocational Course and latterly on the BPTC course where she also had a responsibility for ensuring The City Law School's compliance with Bar Standards Board requirements. Recently retired from The City Law School, Gillian nevertheless has continuing involvement with City's BPTC civil assessments in all of the knowledge and skills areas at both formative and summative stages.

In addition to writing and marking final assessments for LLB, GDL, LPC, BVC and BPTC programmes and supervising dissertations at LLM level, Gillian has also trained professional legal course external examiners. She is therefore well placed to provide advice and guidance on how to pass assessments at all levels of legal education.

Abbreviations

A	Applicant
AC	Appeal Court; the higher court in relation to a lower court
ADR	Alternative Dispute Resolution (ReDOC); see also the definition in GL
AN	Appellant's notice
AOS	Acknowledgment of Service of a document by the party on whom it was served
BPTC	The Bar Professional Training Course
BSB	Bar Standards Board; e.g. a reference in this book to BSB 1.3 is a reference to the third bullet point of section 1 of the required content for the centrally set assessment in civil litigation and evidence ("the syllabus") and hence to the allocation of business between the High and County courts (in outline).
C	Claimant
CA	Court of Appeal
CF	Claim Form
CPR	The Civil Procedure Rules (set out in the White Book)
CRU	Compensation Recovery Unit
D	Defendant
D1	First Defendant
D2	Second Defendant
DBA	Damages-Based Agreements (a contract for legal adviser fees to amount to a percentage amount based on the damages awarded to a client)
ECHR	European Convention on Human Rights
GL	The Glossary in Section F, Volume 1 of the White Book; this abbreviation is used as a helpful indicator within the text of the White Book to alert you to the fact that there is a definition in the glossary
He	All masculine nouns and pronouns should be construed as if they were alternatively feminine nouns and pronouns
HMRC	Her Majesty's Revenue and Customs
HRA	Human Rights Act 1998
JR	Judicial Review

LC	Lower Court
MOCS	**MO**st **C**oncise **S**ummary (distillation of main points to the most basic in order to aid preliminary understanding; found at the end of most chapters)
MCQ	Multiple Choice Question; there are likely to be 40 of this type of question forming part of your Civil Litigation, Evidence and Remedies assessment.
NOCR	No Other Compelling Reason (summary judgment)
NRPOS	No Real Prospect of Succeeding (summary judgement)
PD	Practice Direction (usually found at the end of each part of the CPR)
PI	Personal Injury
POC	Particulars of Claim; a statement of case setting out the details (particulars) of the claim being brought
Provider	The teaching institution who is providing your tuition for the BPTC course
PSLA	Pain, Suffering and Loss of Amenity; one of the measures of damage in PI cases
QBD	The Queen's Bench Division of the High Court
QOCS	Qualified One-Way Cost Shifting
R	Respondent
ReDOC	**RE**solution of **D**isputes **O**ut of **C**ourt (ADR)
RN	Respondent's Notice
RP	Relevant Period for Part 36 offers. (in the chapter on "offers to settle").
RPOS	Real Prospect Of Success (setting aside default judgement); (Appeals)
RTA	Road Traffic Accident
RTA protocol	Pre-Action Protocol for Low Value Personal Injury Claims in Road Traffic Accidents
S.	Section number (of an Act)
SAQ	Short Answer Question; there are likely to be five of this type of question forming part of your Civil Litigation, Evidence and Remedies assessment
She	All feminine nouns and pronouns should be construed as if they were alternatively masculine nouns and pronouns
SOCR	Some Other Compelling Reason (Appeals)
SOGR	Some Other Good Reason (setting aside default judgment)

TIB	Trustee in bankruptcy
TP	Third Party
W	Witness
WB	The White Book; references are to volume 1 unless otherwise stated. Please refer to Appendix Two in this book.
X	A party named X
XIC	Examination In Chief (questioning your own witness); see also the definition in GL
XX	Cross examination (questioning a witness for the other side); see also the definition in GL
Y	A party named Y

For ease of learning, each chapter is organised in the same manner. Each chapter has a heading which is organised in the following way:

Chapter 1

a) Introductory

ORGANISATIONAL MATTERS [BSB 1, CPR Part 1, Part 2 PDs 2B, 2C, Part 3]

The sessions dealing with this area of the syllabus on my BPTC course are	

BSB 1.1   The organisation of the High Court (in outline)

The small letter a) refers to the stage in the progress of a claim dealt with in chapter 1. It is taken from the pictorial outline of a claim set out in the Flow Chart which begins on the next page of this book.

The next line written in upper case imitates the name given to the equivalent relevant section of the required content (syllabus) for the centrally set assessment in Civil Litigation, Evidence and Remedies for the BPTC as set by the Bar Standards Board ("BSB"). The required content is in the BPTC Handbook. You can access a copy in the BPTC Handbook on the BSB website. The required content is reproduced in Appendix Four of this book.

So in our example, Organisational Matters appear in section 1 of the BSB syllabus, shown in the square brackets as [BSB 1.....] The remainder of the square bracket shows the parts of the CPR relevant to this area. Where it is helpful for learning purposes to include specific reference to the CPR numbering, this has been included in the body of the text, although you need not learn the numbering for your BPTC knowledge assessment.

There is then a box for your own cross referencing of the topic with your BPTC course. The meat of the chapter then begins. In this instance it is a subheading which correlates exactly to the wording of the BSB syllabus. Hence both the BSB numbering and wording are all in bold.

I have typed all references to the BSB numbering of the syllabus in bold to make them easy to identify. I have also always used the wording from the BSB syllabus in the body of the book, although if this wording is not in bold, it does not constitute a subheading in its own right.

To help with the process of understanding, I have made all claimants masculine and all defendants feminine (although this could just as easily have been the other way around!)

FLOW CHART

The progress of a claim in the civil courts from pre-action through to trial and beyond

This flow chart reflects procedural situations and considerations at the first possible point in the process that they may occur or are likely to occur.

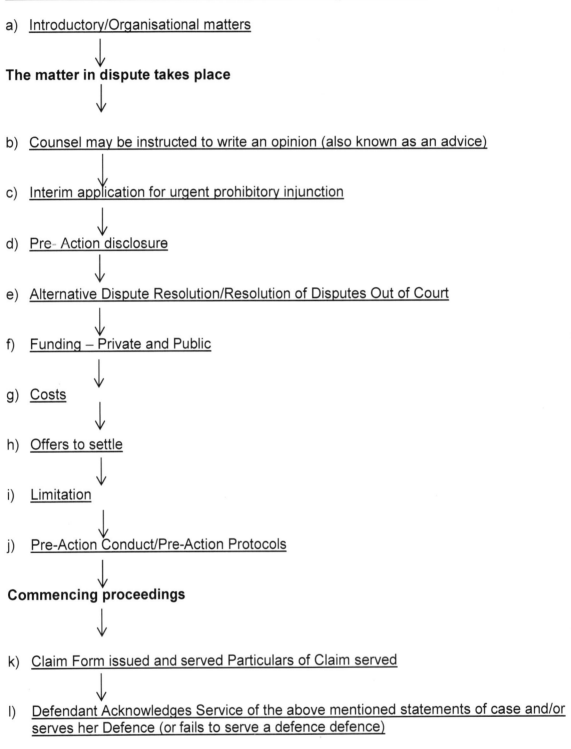

a) Introductory/Organisational matters

↓

The matter in dispute takes place

↓

b) Counsel may be instructed to write an opinion (also known as an advice)

↓

c) Interim application for urgent prohibitory injunction

↓

d) Pre- Action disclosure

↓

e) Alternative Dispute Resolution/Resolution of Disputes Out of Court

↓

f) Funding – Private and Public

↓

g) Costs

↓

h) Offers to settle

↓

i) Limitation

↓

j) Pre-Action Conduct/Pre-Action Protocols

↓

Commencing proceedings

↓

k) Claim Form issued and served Particulars of Claim served

↓

l) Defendant Acknowledges Service of the above mentioned statements of case and/or serves her Defence (or fails to serve a defence defence)

↓

m) <u>D may want to add an additional claim to the original main claim, passing on liability to someone else</u>

    a. Counterclaim against C
    b. Ask for contribution or indemnity against, e.g. D2
    c. "some other remedy" additional claim, e.g. D bringing her own claim against a third party

↓

If parties wish to stop proceedings for a while or discontinue them

n) <u>Stays or Discontinuance</u>

↓

Where statements of case need to be amended

↓

o) <u>Amending statements of case</u>

<u>Next there may be the "what-ifs" – interim applications – set out "in the rim" of the frame on the next page; if none of these is applicable, the case continues with p) track allocation on the page following the "what-ifs".</u>

The "what-ifs" – interim applications

The Defendant

i. **What if D thinks there are no reasonable grounds for bringing the claim?**

   - Apply for strike out and /or
   - Apply for summary judgment (also available to C)

ii. **What if D needs more information (when she sees the claim form and the particulars of claim)?**

   - Request further information

iii. **What if D has concerns that C will not be able to afford to pay D's costs when/if D wins? (Also applies to a person in a defendant position e.g. a claimant when a defendant is counterclaiming against that claimant)**

   - Apply for security for costs

The Claimant

iv. **What if C wants to claim an advance payment of what he believes he will win in damages?**

   - Apply for an interim payment

v. **What if the claimant wants an injunction either to stop the defendant doing something or to require the defendant to do something?**

   - Apply for prohibitory injunction
   - Apply for mandatory injunction

p) Track allocation and case management; notice of proposed allocation, directions questionnaire; sanctions for failing to comply with directions

$$\downarrow$$

q) Evidence

   I. Disclosure and inspection of documents (and Privilege)
   II. Witness statements, hearsay, witness summary, depositions, witness summonses
   III. Expert evidence
   IV. Evidence at trial

$$\downarrow$$

r) Trial

$$\downarrow$$

s) Judgments and orders

$$\downarrow$$

t) Enforcement of judgments

$$\downarrow$$

u) Judicial Review

$$\downarrow$$

v) Appeals

This concludes the civil litigation process. We are now ready to follow a claim through from conception to conclusion, including possible appeals.

> *You are **strongly** recommended to become conversant with the contents of the appendices of this book before beginning to work your way through the substantive chapters.*

Chapter 1

a) Introductory

ORGANISATIONAL MATTERS [BSB 1, CPR Part 1, Part 2 PDs 2B, 2C, Part 3]

The sessions dealing with this area of the syllabus on my BPTC course are	

BSB 1.1   The organisation of the High Court (in outline)

There are three High Court Divisions; QBD, Chancery and Family. In these Divisions, interim applications are heard by Masters, trials heard by High Court judges.

The Divisional Court, the Admiralty Court, Commercial Court and Technology and Construction Court are all part of the QBD. However, each does specialised work requiring a distinct procedure that to some extent modifies the CPR. For that reason each publishes its own Guide or Practice Direction, to which reference should be made by parties wishing to proceed in the specialist courts.

BSB 1.2   The organisation of the County Courts (in outline)

– The County Court has a single seal and a single identity to indicate its national jurisdiction. The court houses in which it convenes act as **hearing centres** with court administrative offices attached to them.

– Small claims hearings, interim applications, possession claims and smaller amount trials are presided over by a District Judge.

– A circuit judge conducts County Court trials.

– In the County Court, a claim or application may be started in any County Court hearing centre, unless any rule, practice direction or enactment provides otherwise.

There are some types of proceedings that must be started in the County Court. Please refer to the table.

Further for claims in the County Court, PD 2C provides an overview of those claims or applications which must be started, or, in some cases, heard, in particular County Court hearing centres, or which may be sent to another hearing centre if started elsewhere. (There are designated County Court hearing centres for probate claims, Technology and Construction Court claims, intellectual property claims, proceedings under Parts 1 to 11 of the Insolvency Act 1986 and for proceedings under section 67(1) and (2) of the Race Relations Act 1976).

If a claim has not been started in the appropriate County Court hearing centre, then, following issue, the claim or application will be **sent** to the appropriate County Court hearing centre in accordance with the relevant rules and practice directions relating to those proceedings before it is issued.

Activity	Have a look at the directory in PD 2C in the White Book. You will see, for example, that there is a County Court Hearing Centre in Aberystwyth which is co-located at a District Registry. The CIVIL TRIAL CENTRE TO WHICH CASES ALLOCATED TO THE MULTI -TRACK WILL BE TRANSFERRED from Aberystwyth is Swansea. Aberystwyth is a County Court Hearing Centre designated as one of the hearing centres where insolvency proceedings and Company and Limited Liability Partnerships proceedings must be started.

- All **money only claims** made under Part 7 of the CPR (detail on Part 7 claims is dealt with in chapter 11 of this book) are processed at one of the two business centres. These are The **County Court Money Claims Centre** in Salford (where money is the only remedy sought) or the **Production Centre at the County Court Business Centre** in Northampton (where money is the only remedy sought and the claimant is a bulk user of the County Court – e.g. a company which offers services to millions of people and so may need to pursue lots of them through the court for payment).

There is also a **Money Claim Online** scheme for money claims with a value of up to the £100,000 threshold for a County Court claim, where neither party is a child or protected party (plus other conditions set out in PD 7E). Claims using this scheme must be sent **electronically**. Any other document, application or request, other than one which is filed electronically must be sent to the County Court Business Centre in Northampton.

BSB 1.3   The allocation of business between the High and County Courts

County Court	High Court
	High value, complex, public interest
Enforcement of Consumer Credit Act agreements	
Damages, specified sum < £100k (not including interest)	Damages, specified sum > £100k (not including interest)
PI < £50k (not including interest or costs)	PI > £50k (not including interest or costs)
	Libel, slander (there is now no presumption of trial with a jury. This is in the judge's discretion at the first case management conference).
	Administrative court of QBD for JR; Planning Court of QBD for planning related JR or statutory challenge; Admiralty; Commercial; Technology and Construction ("TCC")
Chancery business (e.g. land; trusts in some cases <£30k, in others <£350k)	Chancery Division (e.g. land; trusts in some cases >£30k, in others >£350k)

BSB 1.4   The allocation of business between tracks

Courts will allocate a claim to one of the 3 different tracks. These are
- Small claims track, for small claims (!)
- Fast track, for medium-sized claims
- Multi-track for larger claims.

More detail about these tracks appears in the chapters on costs and track allocation.

BSB 1.5   The overriding objective of the Civil Procedure Rules

The overriding objective of the CPR is **to enable the court to deal with cases justly and at proportionate cost**, so that matters are conducted in a quick, cheap and proportionate way. Briefly put, cases must be dealt with in ways which are proportionate with regard to

- Money (the amount involved and the financial position of each party)
- importance
- complexity.

It is imperative, however, that you fully appreciate the importance of this overriding objective and that you address your mind to it constantly from now on. Therefore

> **Activity**   In the White Book, read CPR 1.1 – 1.4 inclusive (just the bold bits);
>
> Note here the exact words that the CPR uses to express the overriding objective in CPR 1.1.

BSB 1.6   The impact of the Human Rights Act on civil claims

The Human Rights Act 1998 brought the European Convention on human rights into effect in the UK. Article 6, (the right to a fair hearing), Article 8, (the right to respect for private and family life) and Article 10, (freedom of expression), are the main Convention provisions impacting on civil claims. Each is dealt with in context later in this book.

Chapter 1 MOst Concise Summary (MOCS)

Whether a claim is to be in the County or High Court and organisation of each court

Overriding objective= justly and at proportionate cost

Human Rights Act has impact

Chapter 2

The matter in dispute takes place

b) Counsel may be asked to write an opinion

REMEDIES, CONTRACT, TORT [BSB 7, 8 and 9]

The sessions dealing with this area of the syllabus on my BPTC course are	

When you are practising the skill of opinion writing on the BPTC, you will be expected to think about (even if you ultimately decide not to include them in your opinion) the areas of law that you have learnt during the academic stage of training. You may be asked to opine on liability (i.e. who is likely, in your opinion, to be liable and whether that person is fully liable or partly liable). Or you may be asked to opine on quantum (i.e. how much is a defendant liable for in money terms); or you may be asked to opine on both liability and quantum.

This chapter sets out some of the basic principles of which you will already be aware and fleshes them out further in concert with the BSB syllabus requirements for remedies, contract and tort.

In addition to the legal concepts, you must learn to opine on practicalities. This means the practical steps to be taken in moving towards the next stage of the litigation process or the next stage of the litigation process itself. It also means setting out in your written opinion any further evidence that you will require in order to opine further together with who would be the best person obtain it.

In accordance with the overriding objective it may be that appropriate advice is for your client to do nothing at this stage, or to wait-and-see, rather than to immediately jump into costly and stress-inducing litigation.

REMEDIES

BSB 7.3   Whether alternative forms of resolving a dispute are available

BSB 7.2   Whether a self-help remedy is available

Do consider these practical alternatives to resolving disputes by litigation. You will learn from your ADR/ReDOC course how important it is to consider these before commencing litigation.

BSB 7.1   The cost of pursuing a remedy; BSB 7.4 The capacity of the defendant to pay damages if awarded

Please wait until you reach the later chapter on costs for the detail of the cost of pursuing a remedy. It is imperative that Counsel focuses both her own mind and that of the client on this. It would be foolhardy or even negligent not to inform the instructing solicitor / lay client of the pros and cons of litigation before they decide on their final instructions to you. Litigation could be an expensive way to resolve a matter that could equally well be resolved, simply by talking to the other side.

There is also little point in pursuing legal remedies if the potential defendant is impecunious and unable to pay damages even if the client is successful.

BSB 7.5   Whether a range of remedies should be pursued

It may be that your academic studies have so far led you to learn topics or modules in isolation. For the vocational stage of training on the BPTC you may therefore need to change the way you attack legal problems. For example it is perfectly common for a party to bring an action against another in both contract and tort.

This is particularly important where some losses in relation to a claim in tort are not reasonably foreseeable. Those losses that are reasonably foreseeable should achieve a remedy. If the claim were brought in tort only, there would be no remedy for any loss which was not reasonably foreseeable. Yet for the same loss there could still be a remedy in contract where it falls within the second limb of Hadley v Baxendale. In such circumstances a claim in tort only would deprive the client of a remedy available to them in contract. More on this follows later in this chapter.

It is always sensible to address your mind to pursuing a range of remedies; for example do your instructions and the facts of the case suggest to you as Counsel a claim for rescission and/or damages in a negligent misrepresentation case?

BSB 7.6   Whether interim remedies should be pursued

Please wait until you reach the later chapters called the "What –ifs".

BSB 7.7   Applicable time limits

Please wait until you reach the later chapter on limitation where applicable time limits are dealt with in context. For now, you should start to be aware that if a situation arises where you need to start a claim again, this may not be possible if the time limit for bringing the claim for this cause of action has already passed.

CONTRACT

BSB 8.1   The general principles underlying damages for breach of contract, including limitations on compensatory damages

General Principles

You will know these general principles from your pre-BPTC studies. Further you will be practising them particularly in the written skill of opinion writing on the course and also in the written skills of drafting statements of case, for example setting out the particulars of your claim. It is therefore imperative that in revising for the civil litigation, evidence and remedies assessment you are studying the subject "in the round" and not simply revising the civil litigation knowledge area of your course as a discrete subject. By analogy, you should be using this civil litigation knowledge to frame a sensible and logical structure in your opinions and statements of case.

The most usual principle is expectation loss, where the claimant ("C") is compensated by being put into the position he would have been in if the contract had been properly performed.

There is also reliance loss, putting C back into the position he was in before the contract was made, perhaps where expectation loss is not easy to assess.

<u>Limitations on compensatory damages:-</u>

<u>Remoteness</u>

Can claim losses naturally arising from breach

The 2 limbs of <u>Hadley</u> v <u>Baxendale</u>

Can claim losses reasonably in the contemplation of the parties. [So when drafting your particulars of claim you need to set out D's knowledge of facts to show that losses claimed were in D's contemplation].

<u>Causation</u>

- What would have happened if there were no breach of contract?
- What did in fact happen?
- What is the difference between the two?
- Did the breach of contract cause this loss?
- What are the consequential losses?

<u>Did C mitigate his loss?</u>

Remember to consider this.

BSB 8.2 The availability of equitable remedies, including specific performance, injunctions, rescission and rectification

Equitable remedies are available only where legal remedies (i.e. damages) are inadequate, provided that the usual bars to equitable remedies are not present e.g. hands must be clean / there must be no delay.

<u>Specific Performance</u>

Not available as a remedy for contracts for personal services, misrepresentation, illegal contracts, obligations entered into voluntarily or needing supervision.

C must be ready, able and willing to perform his own obligations under the contract.

The Court may award C damages in lieu of specific performance.

<u>Injunctions</u>

Orders prohibiting a person from doing something (prohibitory), or requiring a person to do something (mandatory) where there is a related cause of action.

They are available as an interim remedy, i.e. before the cause of action gets to trial. Please wait until you reach the later chapter on interim injunctions.

They are also available as final remedy at trial.

The Court may award damages in lieu of an injunction.

Rescission

Please see the section on misrepresentation below.

Rectification

This is an order to rectify a written record to properly show what the parties intended, where the legal rights between the parties are affected and where the improper record is due to

- a common mistake when drafting the agreement; or
- a mistake by one party that the other party knew about but did not draw to the attention of the first party.

Not available if

- impossible to restore parties to their former positions; or
- judgement debt has been paid already

BSB 8.3   Remedies for misrepresentation

Negligent Misrepresentation

Rescission

To the pre - contract position if no bars to rescission. 'Bars to rescission' means any one of:

- delay;
- restitution is impossible;
- affirmation;
- acquisition of third party rights.

C may be awarded damages in lieu of rescission;

AND / OR

Damages as of right, where they would have been claimable in fraudulent misrepresentation,

- To put C back in the pre - contract position
- For all losses directly flowing from the breach
- C must mitigate his losses.

Fraudulent Misrepresentation

Rescission (note that there is no damages in lieu of rescission); or
Damages

- To put C back in the pre-contract position
- For all losses directly flowing from the breach
- C must mitigate his losses; or

Rescission and Damages

Innocent misrepresentation

Rescission; or damages in lieu of rescission

BSB 8.4 **The law and practice in respect of interest on judgment debts pursuant to contract or statute (Judgments Act 1838; County Court (Interest on Judgment Debts) Order 1991; Late Payment of Commercial Debts (Interest) Act 1998).**

Please wait until you reach the later chapter called Trial.

TORT

BSB 9.1 **The general principles underlying the amount of damages the calculation of quantum, the reduction of damages**

General principles

C is compensated by being put, as closely as can be, into the position he would have been in had the tort not occurred.

Remoteness

C can claim whatever is reasonably foreseeable.

Causation

- What would have happened if there were no breach of the duty owed?
- What did in fact happen?
- What is the difference between the two?
- Did the tort mostly cause this loss (the "but for" test)?

Contributory Negligence

This is where C has contributed to the damage he suffered in relation to a tort by another, for example in a car crash it may not totally be the defendant's ("D"'s) fault that she crashed into C if C suddenly switched lanes.

When calculating quantum, the court will consider the extent to which the actions or omissions of each party caused the accident and the proportion of blame that should be attached to each party.

It could be that the court finds D to be 80% at fault and C 20% at fault. If the court then finds that on full liability D should pay £10,000 inclusive of interest to C, then due to the contributory negligence of C, that amount will be reduced by 20% so that C will receive £8,000 in damages from D.

Did C mitigate his loss ?

Remember to consider whether C has done all he reasonably can to reduce the loss that he has suffered.

BSB 9.1   Aggravated and exemplary damages

Aggravated Damages

Activity Copy out here the definition of aggravated damages from the Glossary in the back of the White Book ("GL"):-

Drafting rule:- plead aggravated damages specifically and separately in the statement of case containing your particulars of claim.

Exemplary Damages

Activity Copy out here the definition of exemplary damages from GL:-

BSB 9.1   The availability of injunctions

Please refer to the subheading 'injunctions' in the section called 'contract' earlier in this chapter. The same is the case where the cause of action is in tort.

BSB 9.2   The principles according to which damages are quantified in PERSONAL INJURY

C is compensated by being put, as closely as can be, into the position he would have been in had the injury not occurred.

Damages for personal injury are quantified by totalling up the following sums for General Damages and Special Damages.

- General damages (losses which are not accurately quantifiable)
  - Pain, Suffering and Loss of Amenity (PSLA)
  - Disadvantage on the labour market; i.e. due to injury C cannot earn as much as previously (a <u>Smith</u> v <u>Manchester</u> award)
  - Loss of pension rights; i.e. if C has to lose or change jobs because of the injury

- Special Damages (accurately quantifiable losses between injury and trial)
  - Damages for past losses + interest on those damages
  - Damages for future losses (no interest)
  - Compensation Recovery Unit deductions.

BSB 9.2 The process by which a court would arrive at a final figure, and the practical steps to be taken in advising on quantum in cases of PERSONAL INJURY

The court would arrive at a final figure by working out the figures for each of the above heads of loss!

Here are the practical steps

- ### GENERAL DAMAGES

  - PSLA

  1. Consult the Judicial College Guidelines.

     These are renewed every year or so; be sure to check that you are using the most up-to-date guidelines.

     Find the section which most accurately reflects the injury to C. When you have decided on it, check the ones both above and below it so that you can be sure you are in the correct section. This will give you a figure or a range of figures between which the amount of compensation should fall.

  2. Find comparable cases to the one on which you are currently advising.

     Use the reputable online services to do this. Your Provider will lead you to them; and/or refer to the publication referred to as "Kemp & Kemp" (short for Kemp & Kemp Quantum of Damages") either online or in hardcopy.

     Be sure to find cases with a claimant of the same age, gender and with comparable injuries and prognosis to those of your client.

     Ideally find a minimum of 3 cases and do a full comparison of each with the case of your client, working out the differences and similarities between each of the cases so that you can ultimately give an informed opinion about the likely amount of damages to be awarded for PSLA. Remember to extrapolate the award for the PSLA from the total amount awarded in the comparable cases that you find.

  3. The comparable cases you have found will have happened before your current case. You will need to adjust the figure for what will be your informed opinion to update the figures from your comparable cases to current day figures.

For a comparable case decided before March 24th 2000 adjust your figure with a <u>Heil</u> v <u>Rankin</u> uplift. This first updates for inflation from the date of the case to March 23rd 2000. Your Provider will tell you where to find the tables which give you the figures with which to calculate this amount.

Once you have the figure to March 23rd 2000 you need to do a calculation for the second inflation uplift from that date to today's date, working now from the <u>Heil</u> v <u>Rankin</u> uplifted figure.

For a comparable case decided after March 24th 2000 adjust the figure to 31st March 2013 (the day before the Jackson reforms came into effect) and then to current day for inflation by using inflation/retail price index tables (Kemp & Kemp contains these). Again, be careful to make sure that you are only using PSLA figures and not figures for the whole of a final award.

4. Make sure that (1) the figure from the Judicial College Guidelines and (2) the figure for your uplifted informed opinion taken and adjusted from the comparable cases are both in the same ballpark; otherwise you have either chosen the wrong section of the Judicial College Guidelines or you have chosen cases which are not comparable to yours. You will then need to go back to find out where your error has been and resolve it before moving on.

5. For judgements given after 1 April 2013 (the date of the implementation of the Jackson reforms), if C had not entered into a Conditional Fee Agreement (now abolished) before then, then there is a further 10% increase to add to general damages. This principle was confirmed by the Court of Appeal in <u>Simmons</u> v <u>Castle</u> in 2013 and in further case law later in the year.

6. The <u>Simmons</u> v <u>Castle</u> uplift does not, note, effect an uplift for inflation. Once the 10% uplift has been applied, the resulting figure needs to be adjusted for inflation from 1st April 2013 to the current date. The inflation/retail price index tables can be used to do this or some of the online comparable cases show inflation updated to today's date for you. Again, be careful to make sure you are only using PSLA figures from the comparable cases and not figures for the whole of a final award.

BSB 9.4 <u>The law and practice in respect of interest on damages in claims for personal injury - Interest on PSLA</u>

2% per annum from the date of service of the claim form to the date of trial.

The meaning of 'date of service of claim form' will be dealt with in the later chapter called 'commencing proceedings'.

- <u>Disadvantage on the labour market - A Smith v Manchester award</u>

Need to show
- o that there is a **serious risk** that at some point in C's life he will find himself on the open labour market (the risk of **future unemployment** does not have to be as a result of the injuries sustained)
- o C's disability would place him at a disadvantage in comparison with an able-bodied contemporary.
- o Net annual salary x (i.e. multiplied by)(a figure called the multiplier, obtained from tables).

- Loss of pension rights

  C is compensated for loss / reduction in his pension where the injury has meant that he is out of work for a while or that he has had to leave his job entirely.

- **SPECIAL DAMAGES**

A schedule of past and future losses must be included attached to the particulars of claim.

The meaning of 'particulars of claim' will be dealt with in the later chapter called 'commencing proceedings'.

- Damages for past losses + interest

  Remember to consider and apply the rules of remoteness, causation and mitigation.

  You will be able to precisely calculate specific losses such as the cost of car repairs, the cost of medicines, the cost of help with domestic chores.

  Loss of earnings is calculated with regard to what C would have earned had he not been injured, all based on net (take home) salary after deductions from his gross salary for National Insurance, pension contributions and tax. The amount of damages is the difference between what he would have earned and what he has actually earned since the injury.

  BSB 9.4 The law and practice in respect of interest on damages in claims for personal injury - Interest on past losses

  The Lord Chancellor sets, (and may change) a Special Account Rate ("SAR"), which has remained set at 0.5% since 1 July 2009.

  One-off losses have interest at the full SAR from the time of the expense to trial.

  Continuous losses since the accident have interest at half SAR.

- Damages for future losses

  You will need to use the Ogden tables to help calculate these.

1. Find the **multiplicand**. When calculating future loss of earnings, this is net annual salary at the date of trial (use today's date in your calculation).

2. Work out the correct **multiplier** by

   i. consulting the Ogden tables for projected mortality. Use the correct one for C based on gender, age and situation, e.g. where the future loss is for loss of earnings; then by

   ii. finding in that table the mortality multiplier based on age and the currently stipulated 2.5% column. I will call the resultant figure "MM" , short for 'mortality multiplier'; then by

   iii. finding the multiplier for contingencies other than mortality in the Ogden tables. Use the correct one for C based on gender, whether loss is for life/to a pension age, whether C is disabled or not disabled, employed or not employed at the time of the accident and to what level C was educated. I will call this figure "OCM", short for 'other contingencies multiplier'.

    iv. The correct multiplier will therefore be MM x OCM.

3. So multiplicand x multiplier = the starting point in calculating a figure for future loss of earnings. I will call this the "current salary figure".

4. C will need to mitigate his loss by taking employment different to that he had before he was injured; so

    i. in relation to work positions he would now be capable of holding, calculate multiplicand x multiplier in relation to that position, in the same way as above. I will call this the "mitigated salary figure";

    ii. subtract the "mitigated salary figure" from the "current salary figure" to give you the amount payable in damages for loss of future earnings.

BSB 9.4 The law and practice in respect of interest on damages in claims for personal injury - **There is no interest on future losses.**

- Compensation Recovery Unit deductions. **BSB 9.3** The impact of Social Security payments on the assessment of damages

Where C is paid recoverable state benefits to the earliest of settlement / trial / 5 years after the accident caused by D, the State will want to recover those benefits. It is D who will effect this in the following way.

D provides C's details (C's date of birth and National Insurance number will be included in C's particulars of claim) to the Unit and obtains a CRU certificate.

The Court awards the sum payable by D to C.

C receives the full amount of PSLA damages.

The amount of benefits paid to C as stated on the CRU certificate are retained by D from the damages payable to C.

D pays the full amount stated on the certificate to the Department of Work and Pensions. This avoids double recovery by C.

Chapter 2 NO MOCS!

Chapter 3

Depending on what the matter in dispute is, C may want to make an

c) Interim application for an urgent prohibitory injunction

INTERIM INJUNCTIONS ("I") [BSB 18, CPR Part 25 PD25A]

The sessions dealing with this area of the syllabus on my BPTC course are	

BSB 18   Interim Injunctions

Although "interim" means "in the middle of" proceedings, **urgent** applications can be applied for and granted **before proceedings start**. An intended claimant could apply to stop a party from doing something by applying for an urgent prohibitory injunction.

Another example of where the interim application can be made before proceedings start is where it is **otherwise necessary to grant interim remedies to a claimant in the interests of justice.**

Interim prohibitory injunctions will be dealt with in detail in the later chapter called "interim injunctions ("II")". They are mentioned here simply to make the point that this type of injunction can be granted in the pre-action stages.

When an interim prohibitory injunction has been granted the court will direct that a claim be commenced.

Further "interim" applications that a claimant may apply for before proceedings start appear in the next chapter.

Interim remedies may also be granted after judgement has been given.

Chapter 3 MOCS

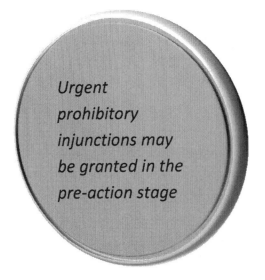

Urgent prohibitory injunctions may be granted in the pre-action stage

Chapter 4

d) Disclosure before proceedings are issued

DISCLOSURE AND INSPECTION OF DOCUMENTS

[BSB15, CPR 31.16. BSB 12, CPR Part 23]

The sessions dealing with this area of the syllabus on my BPTC course are	

BSB 15.1   The law, principles and procedure regulating disclosure and inspection of documents

There are situations where an intended claimant will need documents to be disclosed to him before he issues proceedings to start the litigation process.

[BSB 15.1 disclosure on the BSB syllabus and the other requirements relating to disclosure in the syllabus - 15.2, 15.3 and the second part of 15.5 - will be dealt with in the later chapter called disclosure, in the context of disclosure of documents between parties during the litigation process.]

BSB 15.4   Norwich Pharmacal orders (Norwich Pharmacal Co v Commissioners of Customs and Excise [1974] AC 133)

A potential claimant can apply to court for one of these orders where they want to discover the identity of the potential defendant. This is possible where C wants an order for the **facilitator of the wrong doing** to identify the wrong doer.

For example in an RTA, if one of the drivers does not stop after the accident, yet is driving a car clearly marked as rented from a particular car - hiring company, then C can apply to court for a Norwich Pharmacal order to compel the car hire company to tell him who they rented the car to on that day. C will then have discovered the identity of the defendant.

Note that you can**not** get such an order against a **mere witness** as they did not facilitate the wrong doing.

BSB 15.5   Pre-action disclosure under SCA 1981 s.33 (2) and CPR 31.16 [disclosure against non-parties under SCA 1981 s.34 (2) and CPR 31.17.will be dealt with later in the chapter called "Disclosure and inspection of documents"]

An application to the court for an order for pre-action disclosure is made when a potential claimant needs to look at documents belonging to a potential defendant, to decide whether or not there is a viable case to bring against that potential defendant. The papers must be likely to be or must have been in the **possession, custody or power** of the potential defendant and **relevant to an issue** likely to arise in the claim.

For example if a patient wishes to make a claim against a hospital for poor surgery or care they can apply to court for pre-action disclosure.

The requirements are

- At least a prima facie case

- Both the applicant (potential claimant) and the respondent (potential defendant) must be likely to be a party (i.e. may well be a party), to the ensuing proceedings. There is no need to show that proceedings are likely, though.

- It must be desirable to see these documents now so that
  - proceedings can be avoided,
  - any proceedings will be dealt with fairly,
  - costs can be saved.

- The documents that C is now applying to have disclosed to him must be documents that D would have to disclose to him under standard disclosure during the litigation process.

  Standard disclosure is set out in CPR 31.6.

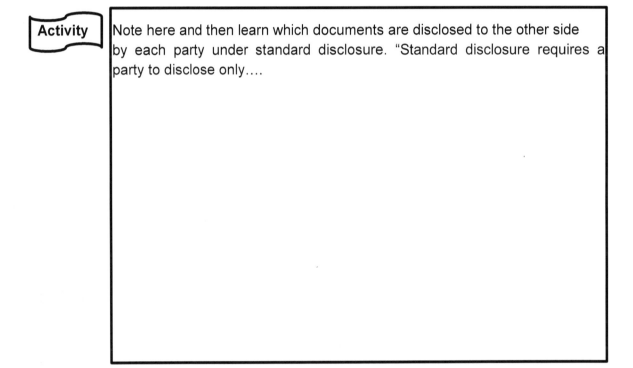

Activity Note here and then learn which documents are disclosed to the other side by each party under standard disclosure. "Standard disclosure requires a party to disclose only....

How to make an application for a Norwich Pharmacal order or for an order for pre-action disclosure. **BSB 12.2** Documentation **required in interim applications**

These applications are made under **Part 23** of the CPR. They are further examples (we have briefly mentioned applications for urgent prohibitory injunctions in the previous chapter) of where interim applications can be made even before proceedings have started. [Interim applications made once proceedings have started are also made under Part 23].

The required documentation is
- Application notice
- Evidence
- A draft of the requested order

APPLICATION NOTICE

- The general rule is that an application must be made to the County Court hearing centre where the claim was started.

  An application made in the County Court **before** a claim has been started may be made at **any County Court hearing centre, unless** any enactment, rule or practice direction provides otherwise.

  So **complete the application notice and get it issued** at the court where proceedings in this matter are **likely to be started**, unless there is good reason to apply to different court.

- **State the order sought and state why it is sought** [When answering the SAQs in the assessment remember to <u>actually state</u> the name of the order sought and <u>why you need it</u> in relation to the scenario about which you are answering the question; <u>applying</u> learned elements of the CPR in your answers is a good thing].

- On issuing, the court inserts the date of the **hearing**, which **must be at least 28 days after the date of the notice.**

- **Serve the notice on the respondent at least 3 clear days before the hearing** of the interim matter; here, the hearing to decide whether or not the Norwich Pharmacal order or order for pre-action disclosure will be given. [So this is a with - notice application i.e. with service of a copy of the application notice to the other side. **BSB 12.1**]

- **BSB 12.3** Calculating periods of notice in interim applications

  - clear days

    - Do not include the beginning day or, where relevant, the day on which an end event occurs

      At least 28 days after the date of the notice.
      Where the date of the notice is the 1st of the month, do not count that date; then count 28 days which takes you to 29th of the month, so the earliest date for the hearing is 30th of the month

      At least 3 clear days before a Friday hearing.
      Do not count Friday, so not Thursday, not Wednesday, not Tuesday. The last date for service is Monday

    - Where the specified period is 5 days or less and includes any of the following, then do not count them in the working out; Saturday, Sunday, a bank holiday, Christmas day or Good Friday

      At least 3 clear days before a Monday hearing.
      Do not count Monday; Sunday and Saturday do not count; then not Friday, not Thursday, not Wednesday, so the last date for service is Tuesday

  - If the court office is closed on the date for service, doing it on the next day the court is open keeps you within the rules.

- The application notice **need not be served** on the respondent (and so would be a 'without notice' application) **where any of the following is the case**
  - there is exceptional urgency
  - the overriding objective is so furthered
  - all parties consent
  - the court gave permission
  - there is not enough time to serve it in the timeframe, so the applicant lets the other side know informally
  - a court order, rule or PD so provides

EVIDENCE

Provide with the application notice **written evidence** which
- must include all material facts
- can be in the application notice itself if it is verified by a statement of truth
- can be in a statement of case which is verified by a statement of truth
- is often a witness statement [including exhibits] verified by a statement of truth

A DRAFT OF THE REQUESTED ORDER

- Attach it to the application notice
- Take a copy of it to the hearing on a disk/digital stick.

Chapter 4 MOCS

Before proceedings are issued,

to discover identity of defendant or

to discover whether you have a viable case,

apply under Part 23:-

- *application notice*
- *written evidence*
- *draft order*

Chapter 5

e) Alternative dispute resolution/resolution of disputes out of court

The sessions dealing with this area of the syllabus on my BPTC course are	

BSB 7.3   Whether alternative forms of resolving a dispute are available (ADR/ReDOC)

 Activity

> You may find it useful to copy the definition of ADR from GL here:-

This is taught and assessed as a complete module in its own right on the BPTC. You should therefore cross refer your notes for that module with the civil litigation, evidence and remedies module. It is strongly advised that you refresh your recall of ADR/ReDOC for the civil litigation, evidence and remedies assessment.

Remember that ADR/ReDOC must be considered, not only at pre-action stages but as appropriate throughout the litigation process.

In addition, the BPTC also contains training and assessment in oral and written skills. Naturally the sessions for these will build on the knowledge you acquire during the civil litigation module. You should not neglect to revise for the assessment in civil litigation, evidence and remedies any additional matters you have also learned in the oral and written skills sessions.

Remember that the assessment syllabus includes knowledge of the areas of contract and tort. If you have not already done so, it would be a good idea to revise your undergraduate/GDL knowledge of these areas together with the contents of chapter 2 of this book.

Civil litigation on the BPTC is not a series of topics to be learned in isolation; it is a whole subject to be viewed in the round.

Chapter 5 MOCS

Remember to revise the ADR / ReDOC Course; remember to revise all civil elements of the BPTC for the civil litigation, evidence and remedies assessment

Chapter 6

f) FUNDING

[BSB 22; Legal Aid Sentencing and Punishment of Offenders Act 2012; Damages- Based Agreement Regulations 2013]

The sessions dealing with this area of the syllabus on my BPTC course are	

BSB 22.1   The nature of private funding

Legal advisers earn a living by being paid for the legal services they provide. The contract between a party and the legal adviser is called a retainer.

The court may order that a loser pays what the winner owes his or her legal adviser(s) (the winner's costs) although this is not always the case.

So if a party loses a case the court may order that therefore that party pays the winner's costs of his or her legal advisers as well as their own.

Or the court may order somewhere in-between where the loser is ordered to pay only part of the winner's costs.

It may be that the court assesses that less is to be paid by way of costs than legal advisers have charged.

Thus there may be times when even a winner needs to privately fund payment to their own legal advisers.

Private funding

BSB 22.1   Before the event insurance

Home or motor insurance companies policies may include insurance for legal expenses. The insurers will ask the lawyers to advise on the merits of a claim to assess whether litigation is justified under the policy.

BSB 22.1   Damages - Based Agreements ("DBA") (not in family cases)

Under DBAs there is an agreement between the client and the legal adviser where what is paid to the legal advisers is based on the damages that the client wins. There is no need to disclose the agreements to the other side, although you can. Such agreements are more likely to be used where a client has **'before the event' insurance.**

The agreement must
- be in writing
- limit the costs of the legal adviser to an agreed percentage of damages awarded to the client
- Set out the % and why it is at that level

For PI this is capped at 25% of the award for pain, suffering and loss of amenity ("**PSLA**") and **past** losses, net of Compensation Recovery Unit payments i.e. 25% inclusive of VAT of what the client is entitled to have received by now.

For other causes of action this is capped at 50% i.e. 50% inclusive of VAT of all sums ultimately recovered by the claimant.

Neither winner nor loser, whoever is ordered to pay the costs, will pay more than the above DBA-capped percentages, even if the judge awards costs to be paid by one party and the legal adviser fees of the other party amount to more than the DBA percentage. For this reason, there are those who feel that DBAs may change as this kind of agreement puts lawyers at too much risk; it could mean that they are unable to recover all their fees.

BSB 22.1 Public funding

This is administered by the Legal Aid Agency. Public finding is **not** available for funding
– Company/partnership matters
– Conveyancing
– Damages for PI/death/clinical negligence (unless the claim regards neo-natal brain injuries)

There is **limited public funding** available for
– employment law
– family law
– housing
– judicial review

There is a **means and merits test** for eligibility
– need at least 50% prospect of success
– for funding for full representation need to show a cost benefit e.g.
   • + 80% prospect of success and damages must be likely to be greater than the costs
   • 60% to 80% prospects of success and damages must be likely to be double the costs
   • 50% to 60% success and damages must be likely to be 4 times the costs.

BSB 22.8 The effects of state funding and the statutory charge on civil litigation and counsel's duty to the Legal Aid Agency; BSB 22.7.3 The likely effect on the order for costs where one or more parties is publicly funded

If publicly funded, you must notify your opponent either during the pre-action protocol, or, at the latest, when issuing the Claim Form.

If you win

– The statutory charge comes into operation
   • funding is a loan not a gift
   • there is a first charge to the Legal Aid Agency for their costs over any money (i.e. damages) / property recovered or preserved from the litigation); so
   • if the court orders that the loser pays the winner's costs but the fees of the Legal Aid Agency are more than the court orders to be paid, the winner makes up the shortfall from the damages recovered.

If you lose

– the client has costs protection
   • The court can only order a publicly funded litigant to pay what is reasonable with regard to all the circumstances of the case. This will include consideration of the parties' financial situation and the conduct of parties towards the case. So a losing publicly funded client will often pay nothing.

- Rarely will the Lord Chancellor (i.e. The Legal Aid Agency) be ordered to pay the costs of a privately funded winning D. It is only likely to arise if it is just and equitable to do so and D would be in financial hardship otherwise.

Chapter 6 MOCS

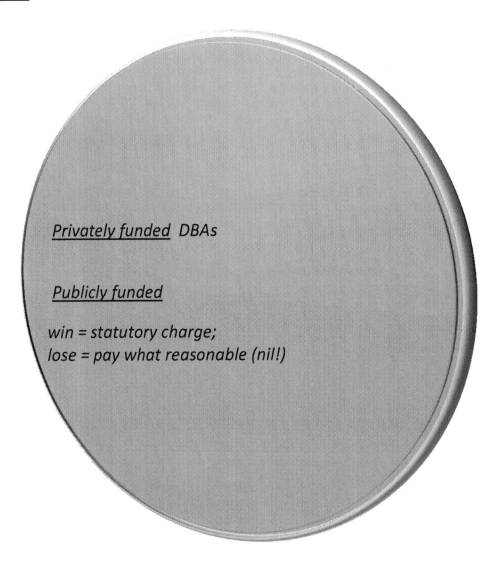

Privately funded DBAs

Publicly funded

win = statutory charge;
lose = pay what reasonable (nil!)

Chapter 7

g) COSTS

[BSB 22, 14; CPR 3.1, 3.12, 3.14, PD 3E, Part 44, particularly rules 44.3; 44.6; 44.7;

Part 45, Part 36]

The sessions dealing with this area of the syllabus on my BPTC course are	

General principles

Costs is the amount that a client pays to their legal advisers.

The likely amount of costs and who may have to pay them should have an important bearing when deciding whether or not to litigate, before any litigation is started.

At the end of a hearing or trial the court will draw up an order. When an order is silent as to costs no party is entitled to costs; each party therefore pays their own legal advisers' costs. Counsel must therefore ask for an order for costs once judgement has been given.

The court has discretion as to costs.

Methods of assessing costs

BSB 22.3   The different methods of assessing costs (summary and detailed assessment) and when each is appropriate

Not applicable to small claims as legal adviser costs are not normally awarded.

Summary assessment (not where litigants are publicly funded)

The court determines costs there and then at the end of the hearing or trial after judgement has been given.

Usually for
- one-day long interim application hearings; a short statement of costs must be served 24 hours before the hearing
- fast track trials; a short statement of costs must be served 2 days before the hearing.

Failure to serve a statement of costs could mean
- adjournment for a short period to allow the losing party to consider a late statement of the winner's costs. In this case the Judge would consider the summary assessment with added leniency towards the losing, paying party; or
- adjournment to a later date for summary assessment before the same judge or for summary assessment in writing; or
- adjournment for further, detailed assessment.

Detailed assessment

For
- interim application hearings of more than one day
- multi-track cases

where there is a dispute about the amount of costs claimed, the court can order detailed assessment by a costs officer.

The disputing party needs to commence proceedings by serving notice of commencement for an appeal of costs within 3 months of any of the following
- final judgement
- end of the claim by discontinuance [You will learn about this way of ending a claim later in this book].
- end of the claim by acceptance of a part 36 offer. [You will learn about this way of ending a claim later in this book].

The court may order the paying party to pay a reasonable sum on account of costs before the detailed assessment so that the winning party's legal advisers get at least some payment straight away.

Who pays whose costs?

The starting point is that **loser pays winner** (i.e. **costs follow the event**); the court has discretion and so may make a different order.

In using its discretion the court has regard to all circumstances
- the level of success of the winner
- any offers to settle already made (not Part 36 ones - see later in this chapter)
- how the parties have conducted themselves pre (including protocol adherence) and per proceedings
- the reasonableness of the parties' allegations
- the way the parties pursued the allegations
- whether the successful C has exaggerated his claim

So it may be that the **loser pays winner principle may be adjusted** in the court's discretion, with the loser paying anything in the range between none or all of the winner's costs, as well as paying their own legal advisers' costs as the loser.

Costs are to be paid within 14 days of judgement if the amount of costs is stated. If there is a further detailed assessment of costs, the assessment may state the date when payment should be made, or the court may specify when payment should be made.

BSBS 22.8 The power of the courts to make a costs order in favour of the Access to Justice Foundation in a pro bono case (Section 194 of the Legal Services Act 2007; CPR 46.7(4)

Where lawyers are working purely out of goodwill, not charging a client, they are said to be working "**pro bono**".

Pro bono costs are just like ordinary legal costs, but where a party has free legal representation. If a civil case is won with pro bono help, pro bono costs can be ordered by the court, or included in settlements. The court can make a costs order which provides that the losing party pays the amount that the winner's costs would have been with respect to any period when free representation was provided.

Payment will be to the prescribed charity, the **Access to Justice Foundation**, which distributes the money to agencies and projects that give free legal help to those in need.

How much is to be paid?

In some cases costs are fixed at a certain amount (**fixed costs**). These are set out in the tables in part 45 CPR.

For example (I), Tables 1 and 2 identify the fixed costs in the case where the claim is for a specified sum of money over £25 and where

- Default Judgment is obtained; or
- the defendant makes an admission; or
- the defence is struck out as there are no reasonable grounds for defending the claim; or
- Summary Judgment is given (do not mix up in your mind summary assessment of costs and summary judgment; remember that summary simply means "there and then".

The detail of Default Judgment, Summary Judgment and striking out will be dealt with in later chapters.

The above four situations will have further fixed costs payable if the situations in Table 4 of part 45 have arisen. [Please wait until later in the chapter called "commencing proceedings" where personal service, alternative method and alternative place of service are dealt with].

For example (II), (and please note that chapter 10 in this book introduces Pre-Action Protocols)

Fixed costs apply where a claim begins under either the Pre-Action Protocol for Low Value Personal Injury Claims in Road Traffic Accidents or the Pre-Action Protocol for Low Value Personal Injury (Employers' Liability and Public Liability) Claims (unless it is a disease case), but is no longer continuing under that Protocol.

A claim will be subject to the Pre-Action Protocol for Low Value Personal Injury Claims in Road Traffic Accidents when, on a full liability basis including pecuniary losses but excluding interest, the claim is no more than

- £25,000 where the accident occurred on or after 31 July 2013; or
- £10,000 where the accident occurred on or after 30 April 2010 and before 31July 2013.

Claims no longer continue under the low value protocols when

- parties reach a settlement prior to the claimant issuing proceedings under Part 7; or
- proceedings are issued under Part 7, but the case settles before trial; or
- the claim is disposed of at trial.

There is a table of fixed costs for each of the two protocols, escalating according to how far the claim has proceeded, set out in CPR 45.29A (Section IIIA of Part 45).

BSB 22.4   The different bases on which costs are assessed (standard and indemnity)

Any costs unreasonably incurred or of an unreasonable amount will not be allowed.

Where there is no reference in a costs order to either the standard basis or the indemnity basis, the basis of assessment will be the standard basis.

The **standard basis** is the most usual way for the costs for the legal adviser of the receiving winner to be assessed. This is the case when those costs have been reasonably incurred, are of a **reasonable** amount, and are **also proportionate**.

If there is any doubt about whether or not the winning party's costs are reasonable and proportionate, any residual doubt will be resolved in favour of the paying loser, so that at worst the costs of the receiving party could be disallowed. Here the court will have regard to

- the conduct of the parties pre-and per proceedings
- efforts made to resolve the case
- the value and importance to the parties, the complexity of the case, time spent and work done on the case
- for multi-track cases, the amount agreed in the final costs budget [more on this later in this chapter].

The **indemnity basis** is punitive of the poor conduct of a losing opponent. Any doubt as to the **reasonableness** of the legal adviser costs of the receiving winner (note that there is **no** reference to proportionality) will be made in favour of the winning receiving party (so indemnifying the winning party for the poor conduct of the losing party).

Costs regarding each track.

Small claims track and costs

Claims likely to be allocated to the small claims track are

- <£10k
- PSLA < £1k
- Housing disrepair < £1k

The only **costs** between the parties are

- fixed costs under the RTA protocol,
- court fees, e.g. the court fee payable on issue of a claim form,
- witness travel expenses and loss of earnings
- disbursements up to £750 per expert
- an amount the court assesses where any party has behaved unreasonably.

Fast track and costs

Claims likely to be allocated to the fast track are

- £10k - £25k
- PSLA > £1k*
- Housing disrepair > £1k

- NOT claims by residential tenants re harassment or unlawful eviction by landlord

The **costs** between the parties

- Parties file standard form signed statements of costs not less than 2 days before trial
- as set out above in this chapter. i.e.
  - summary assessment after judgement
  - loser pays winner (court may adjust)
  - fixed costs as in Part 45 CPR re the amount C recovers if acting for C, or re the statement of value on the claim form if acting for D
  - on standard or indemnity basis

* As PSLA refers to PI cases, do remember that "<u>For example (II)</u>" on fixed costs on the previous page has to all intents and purposes introduced fixed costs for fast track claims that began under the Pre-Action Protocol for Low Value Personal Injury Claims in Road Traffic Accidents but are no longer continuing under it. This is because there are many PI RTA claims that fall into this category.

The next paragraph on Multi-track and costs includes detail on costs budgets in costs management. It is worthy of note that as CPR 3.1(2)(II) provides that the court may "order any party to file and exchange a costs budget", it is possible that costs budgets could be ordered on the fast track too. The PD on case management provides that in all cases the court will have regard to the need for litigation to be conducted justly and at proportionate cost in accordance with the overriding objective.

Multi-track and costs

Claims likely to be allocated to the multi-track are

- £>25K
- Claims of real public importance
- Part 8 claims (These are explained in chapter 11 of this book.)

BSB 14.4 <u>The impact of costs and the role of costs budgets in case management.</u>

The purpose of costs management is that the court should manage both the steps to be taken and the costs to be incurred by the parties to any proceedings so as to further the overriding objective.

<u>First</u>, where the claim is commenced on or after 22nd April 2014 costs management does **not** apply to some Part 7 multi-track claims, although the PD on costs management provides that the court does nevertheless have discretion to make an order requiring parties to those claims to file cost budgets.

Costs management does not apply to those Part 7 multi-track claims which are
- subject to fixed costs; nor
- subject to scale costs (these are used in intellectual property claims),
- >£10million
- stated to be valued at >£10million, although no full quantification has been given.

In these cases, at an early stage in the litigation the parties should consider and, where practicable, discuss whether to apply for an order for the provision of costs budgets, with a view to a costs management order being made. The PD sets out situations where this may be appropriate, e.g. personal injury and clinical negligence cases where the value of the claim is £10 million or more. If all parties consent to an application for an order for provision of costs budgets, the court will (other than in exceptional cases) make such an order.

<u>Secondly</u>, otherwise, cost management **does** apply to Part 7 multi-track cases, including applications, unless the court orders otherwise.

Parties (except where a litigation friend is appointed for them - more on this later in chapter 12) prepare and file detailed **costs budgets.**

They must be verified by a statement of truth, the wording for a statement of truth verifying a budget is set out in Practice Direction 22, note 2.2A, "This budget is a fair and accurate statement of incurred and estimated costs which it would be reasonable and proportionate for my client to incur in this litigation".

The contents of the costs budgets are recorded by the court. The court will be in a position to consider making a costs management order.

If the parties have not managed to agree the budgets, then the court reviews them, makes appropriate revisions <u>then records</u> the extent of such agreement together with its approval of the budgets. If the court does not approve the costs budgets, e.g. where the cost budgets are disproportionate as they exceed the value of the claim, the court cannot make a costs management order.

When budgets are approved, the court makes a **costs management order** in respect of costs to be incurred in the future.

Courts use the budgets to manage the case and make decisions, considering whether the budgeted costs fall within the range of **reasonable and proportionate** costs and the steps that parties will be ordered to take to prepare for trial.

Parties can **file amended** budgets as the case proceeds, for **court** consideration and **approval.** The court can convene a hearing for this, called a costs management conference, though approval should preferably be done by phone or in writing.

If a party does not file a budget, the sanction is that he or she is taken to have filed one which deals only with the applicable court fees. Courts will not depart from approved/agreed costs budgets when making orders as to costs at the end of the trial unless satisfied there is a good reason to do so. (The Courts do seem to be applying this to the letter, refusing to grant relief from this sanction).

The criteria which the court considers on an application for replying for relief from this (or any) sanction are set out in CPR 3.9. Full details are in chapter 22 of this book.

At the end of the trial, the winner's recoverable **costs will be assessed by reference to the last approved budgets**.

BSB 22.7   <u>The likely effect on the order for costs where a party achieves only partial success</u>

<u>Example 1- percentage success order</u>

C brings a claim against D, D makes a counterclaim against C (usually in relation to the claim that C brought although it does not have to be). If C wins, say, £4k on the original claim and then D wins, say, £5k on a counterclaim, then overall D has won £1k in damages/compensation. £1k is 20% of what D claimed. With the percentage success order C will pay 20% of the costs and as to the remaining 80% the parties will bear their own costs.

<u>Example 2</u> is on the next page.

<u>Example 2</u>   **BSB 22.7.2 - the likely effect on the order for costs where there is a joinder of defendants and the claimant succeeds against some but not all of them**

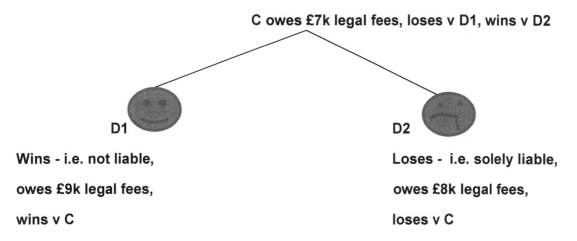

C owes £7k legal fees, loses v D1, wins v D2

D1

Wins - i.e. not liable,

owes £9k legal fees,

wins v C

D2

Loses - i.e. solely liable,

owes £8k legal fees,

loses v C

<u>Example 2.1 Bullock order</u>

- Where it was reasonable for C to bring the case against more than one D
- Bullock orders are very common
- This achieves indirect payment to protect a winning D, ensuring she gets her costs;
  - the losing C pays the costs of the winning D and C is reimbursed by the losing D
  - the losing D then pays the winning C's costs.
  (If it were simply loser pays winner, C would not be so reimbursed; the court may still make such a 'loser pays winner' order if it did not consider it reasonable for C to bring the case against more than one D).

- So a Bullock order would mean

1]   C loser pays costs (i.e. legal fees) of D1 winner

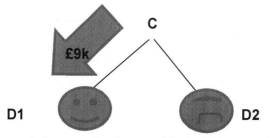

2]   D2 loser reimburses C winner with the amount of D1 costs

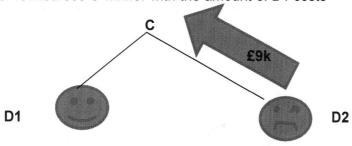

3]   D2 loser pays C winner costs

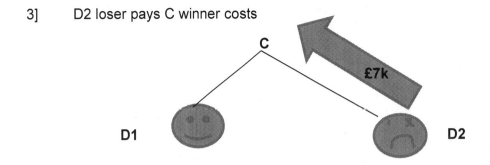

Example 2.2 Sanderson order

- Again, for where it was reasonable for C to bring the case against more than one D
- Sanderson orders are not so common, used e.g. if C publicly funded or insolvent
- It means that a publicly funded/insolvent C has no obligation to pay the winning D1 – it is D2 who pays D1

- So a Sanderson order would mean

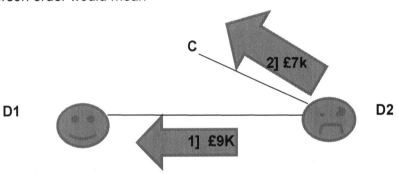

1] Losing D pays winning D's costs

2] Losing D pays winning C's costs

BSB 22.1   Qualified one-way costs shifting (QOCS)

This is relevant in a **PI / death / fatal accident case where the claimant is the loser.**

Even though the general principle of loser pays winner may be followed, (i.e. by the court making a costs order in favour of the winning D), the winning D can enforce payment of the winning D's costs against the losing C **only up to the amount that the losing C has been awarded in damages and interest.** [Thus a losing C pays no more in costs than the amount they have won in damages and interest on those damages]. [Situations where a losing C will have been awarded something in damages and interest, thus giving D an amount enforceable as to that winning D's costs, are set out on the next page].

Since it is likely that the losing C will not have been awarded anything in damages and interest, D is not able to enforce against C.

So the costs have been shifted one-way so that enforcement against the losing C is limited/changed/qualified as to the amount they will have to pay of the winning D's costs; limited, that is, to the amount C has won in damages and interest.

The costs order in favour of the winning D is not treated as an unsatisfied judgement against the losing C.

Situations where a losing C will have been awarded something in damages and interest, thus giving D an amount enforceable as to that winning D's costs, are

- where C has had a partial success and has therefore been awarded some damages and interest
- where C wins (and so has been awarded some damages and interest) but has failed to obtain judgement more advantageous than a D's part 36 offer [for explanation and details of this see the next chapter].

Situations where QOCS does not apply, so that a losing D can still enforce to the full extent even though the C is a loser in a PI / death / fatal accident case

- D wins strike out [See later in chapter 16] on the grounds that
  - C disclosed no reasonable grounds for bringing proceedings; or
  - the proceedings are an abuse of the court's process; or
  - the conduct of C or someone acting on C's behalf with C's knowledge is likely to obstruct the just disposal of the proceedings.

- With court permission where on the balance of probabilities the claim is found to be fundamentally dishonest.

BSB 22.6   The situations where costs orders do not follow the event

- Where the court has used its discretion not to give such an order
- The costs of some interim applications [a later chapter deals with such applications]
- Example 1 [BSB 22.7] above. (If costs did follow the event it is likely that the losing D on the original claim would have more costs to pay than would the losing C on the counterclaim, even though overall D has won more damages)
- Examples 2.1 and 2.2 [BSB 22.7] above
- Enforcement in a QOCS case [BSB 22.1] above
- Under certain circumstances where there has been a Part 36 offer to settle. See next chapter, scenario (ii).

Chapter 7 MOCS

Please see the next page.

Costs are in the court's discretion

Assessed summarily/detailed

Courts may adjust "loser pays winner"

Some costs are Part 45 fixed

Costs payable on standard or indemnity basis

Costs on Small/Fast tracks

Costs on multi track = costs budgets and costs management

Percentage success orders

Bullock = C pays winning D and is reimbursed by losing D

Sanderson = all payments by losing D

QOCS

Where costs do not follow the event

Chapter 8

h) OFFERS TO SETTLE

[BSB20; CPR Part 36:- particularly rules 36.2; 36.3(3); 36.10(1),(3); 36.10(4), 36.10A; 36.14, 36.14A]

The sessions dealing with this area of the syllabus on my BPTC course are	

General outline and background to Part 36

Dealing with costs can become a very tactical matter.

Part 36 is a formalised system to motivate parties to agree to acceptable offers to settle a claim and so avoid the need to go through proceedings to trial. A party may make an offer at any time, even before proceedings are started.

There are cost penalties (i.e. the costs of proceeding onwards to an unnecessary trial) for those who don't accept acceptable offers, then fail to obtain judgement for an amount more advantageous at trial than was earlier offered to them.

BSB 20.1   The requirements in making offers to settle under Part 36

Form and content of an offer

- In writing
- Stating part 36 intentions
- Stating whether the offer relates to the whole or part of the claim
- Stating whether it takes into account a counterclaim
- Specifying at least a 21 day period where if C (the offeree) accepts the offer during this period, thus making C the winner, then the loser (the offeror) D pays the C's winner's costs and the claim is at an end; please see further the activity box below about this, the **relevant period.**

If the offer is invalid for wrong form or content, the court will still include knowledge of it when considering what order to make as to costs.

BSB 20.2   Calculation of the relevant period [CPR 36.3(1) (c)]

Activity

Refer to CPR 36.3(1) (c) in the White Book and note it here, to help you understand the definition of the relevant period ("RP")

Relevant period means in the case of an offer made NOT less than 21 days before a trial, the period specified under rule 36.5(1)(c) or such longer as the parties agree otherwise, the period up to the end of such trial

Now see this further under BSB 20.3 and depicted in diagram form under BSB 20.4 below

---

21 days before the trial you can't so make a pt 36 offer. Can 22 days or even 21 days up to trial & until trial ended

Part 36 offers include interest, so a "£500 offer" is [£x plus interest = £500 to the end of the RP]; an offer stays open unless and until it is withdrawn and so interest will continue to accrue. So, to see whether or not C has obtained a judgement more advantageous at trial than was earlier offered to C, one will need to calculate £x + interest to end of RP + accruing interest to date of trial.

Within 7 days of an offer, the offeree may ask for clarification by making a Part 23 application. If granted, the court will specify the date on which the offer is to be treated as made.

BSB 20.6   Secrecy relating to offers to settle, and the consequences of breach.

Judges are not told about the unaccepted offer until liability and quantum have been finalised at the trial, unless all parties agree in writing that he or she may be told. If the secrecy is breached the judge can
- continue with trial if s/he is satisfied that there is no prejudice to either side, having regard to overriding objective; or
- s/he can withdraw from the case.

A Part 36 offer is treated as 'without prejudice except as to costs'. This means that where there is a bona fide attempt to settle in this way, **the court has no knowledge of the offer** but after the trial may take it into account when exercising its discretion as to costs.

BSB 20.3   Consequences of accepting offers to settle under Part 36;

The following steps are taken to accept a Part 36 offer. Note, the non-bold text relates to the period between the offer and the end of the RP. **The bold text relates to the time between the end of the RP and the trial/beyond.**

- The offeree
  - writes to the offeror accepting the offer
  - files notice of acceptance at court
  - serves notice of the acceptance during RP

- D pays all these standard basis costs to the date of the notice of acceptance

  Or the costs will be fixed costs, if the claim began under the RTA Protocol, but is no longer continuing under it. This could be either because the "parties reach a settlement prior to the claimant issuing proceedings under Part 7" (i.e. the offeree accepts the offer before proceedings have been issued), "or [because] proceedings are issued under Part 7, but the case settles before trial" (i.e. the matter has been started in the courts, when the offeree accepts the offer)

- **If the offer is not withdrawn, notice of acceptance can be served after RP**

  Or if the claim began under the RTA Protocol as in the paragraph above, the costs will be fixed costs for the stage applicable at the date on which the relevant period expired; whereas for the period from the end of the relevant period to the date of acceptance, the claimant will be liable for the defendant's costs. (In relation to whiplash cases, if the defendant makes a Part 36 offer before the defendant receives a fixed cost medical report, these cost consequences will only have effect if the claimant accepts the offer more than 21 days after the defendant received the report)

- **Parties agree liability for costs; if not, the court makes an order for costs**

- Notice of acceptance served after trial started needs court permission to be effective
- Notice of acceptance served after trial but before judgment is only effective if the parties agree

Accepting, and BSB 20.4 withdrawing, reducing and increasing Part 36 offers to settle in diagram form

	Trial
<u>RP 21 days or as agreed</u>	<u>Or RP to end of trial if offer made within 21 days trial</u>
D Offeror-- ──────────────►	──────────────────────────►
C ideally accepts offer within RP	**C offeree can accept it after RP until withdrawn**
D can't withdraw/change offer until end RP without court permission. Apply for permission using Part 23 CPR	**D can withdraw/change offer serving notice on offeree without court permission**
Offer accepted = C wins	**Where offer accepted after RP and parties do not agree costs, the usual court order is that the offeree pays the offeror's costs from end RP to acceptance**
So loser pays winner	
D pays all these standard basis costs to the date of the notice of acceptance	
For claims begun under the RTA Protocol these are fixed costs.	**In whiplash claims, where D's offer was made before her receipt of the fixed costs medical report then acceptance after the end of RP means acceptance more than 21 days after D received that report.**
The idea is that C should accept a reasonable offer to avoid cost consequences	
<u>End of RP</u>	<u>Trial</u>

45

Examples of Part 36 scenarios

Note that for simplicity's sake, none of these scenarios includes a claim started under the RTA protocol. You should refer to CPR 36.14A for the consequences for such cases.

In scenarios (i-iii) the parties' costs are

- C's costs to end RP   £18,000
- D's costs to end RP   £20,000
- C's costs from end RP   £53,000
- D's costs from end RP   £58,000

Scenario (i) – C rejects reasonable offer then loses at trial

e.g. D makes an offer of £70k which C rejects. At trial the judge dismisses the claim so
i.e. C loses - 36.14 (1) (a) C fails to obtain judgment more advantageous

In diagram form

C loses as judge dismisses claim i.e. 36.14 (1) (a) C fails to obtain more advantageous.

	End of RP	C loses at trial

£70k offer RP 21 days or more as agreed

D £70k offer ----------------→ ----------------→

General principles, loser pays winner,	**36.14 (2) D entitled to her costs, unless unjust, + interest**
So C pays D's costs to end RP	**so C pays D's costs from end RP**
i.e. loser pays winner on standard basis	**i.e. ("loser pays winner" not re general principles, but re CPR 36.14 (2) on the standard basis**
So C pays D's £20k costs as well as own	**so C pays D's £58k costs as well as own**
Remember if PI, QOCS means D cannot enforce against C to make C pay D's costs!	**Remember if PI, QOCS means D cannot enforce against C to make C pay D's costs!**

End of RP   Trial

Scenario (ii) – C rejects offer then wins at trial but wins the same as or less than D offered

e.g. D makes an offer of £70k which C rejects. At trial the judge awards C £70k or less
i.e. C wins BUT- 36.14 (1) (a) C fails to obtain judgment more advantageous.
i.e. BSB 20.5 Consequences of failing to obtain judgment which is more
advantageous than an offer to settle

In diagram form

C wins same or less than D's offer i.e. 36.14 (1) (a) C fails to obtain judgment more advantageous.

	End of RP	C wins £70k or less at trial
£70k offer RP 21 days or more as agreed		
D £70k offer—		
General principles, loser pays winner,	**36.14 (2) D entitled to her costs, unless unjust, + interest**	
So D pays C's costs to end RP	**So C pays D's costs from end RP**	
i.e. loser pays winner on standard basis **D lost at trial so D pays to end RP**	**i.e. Costs do not follow the event. The idea is that C is penalised in costs for not accepting an offer he should have accepted, paying the costs for the other side for the most expensive bit of the process**	
So D pays C's £18k costs as well as own	**So C pays D's £58k costs as well as own. These figures can be set off against one another so that C would pay £40k costs to D. (58 minus 18).**	
	Remember if PI, that due to QOCS, D can enforce the costs of D that C is to pay, (only) up to C's £70k damages award +interest without court permission. In our example D could therefore enforce against C for the £40k costs.	
	The QOC enforcement position would be different if with the same costs the offer amounted to the same as or less than the trial award to C of £30k + interest. D would still need to fund £several thousands of her own costs. (40 minus [30 + interest]).	
End of RP		Trial

Scenario (iii) – C rejects offer then wins at trial winning more than D offered

e.g. D makes an offer of £70k which C rejects. At trial the judge awards C £90k
i.e. C wins and C DID NOT FAIL to obtain judgment more advantageous

In diagram form

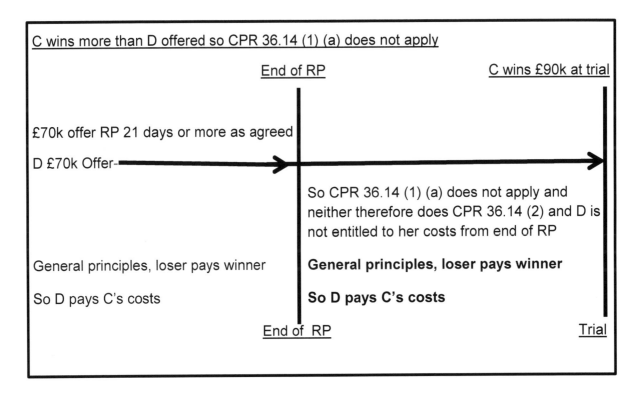

Scenario (iv) – Following the D's £70k offer C makes a COUNTER-OFFER asking D to pay £95k which D rejects. C is awarded £95k or more at trial.

CPR 36.14 (1) (b) judgment is against D and the trial award is at least as advantageous to C as was C's counter offer.

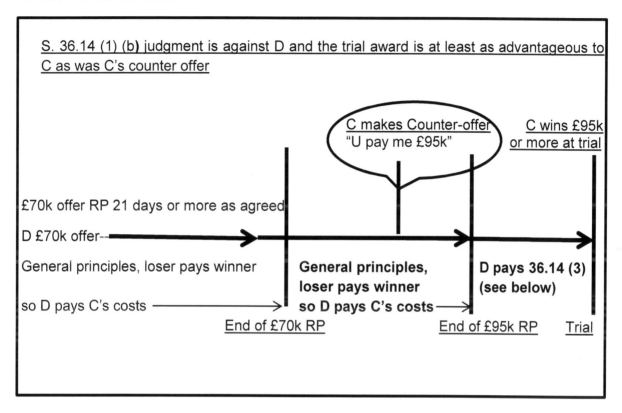

CPR 36.14 (3)
[briefly put, D pays C's final stage costs on the indemnity basis with enhanced interest]

To encourage settlement and avoid a trial, D will have to pay extra amounts to C if he fails to accept an offer he should have reasonably accepted. These are

− Costs on the **indemnity** basis from the end of the counteroffer RP
− Interest on those costs not exceeding 10% above the Bank of England base rate
− Up to 10% above base rate interest on the awarded amount (£800 in this example) from the end of the counteroffer RP - unless unjust
− An additional amount up to £75,000. For monetary or part-monetary claims it is based on a percentage of the award. For non-monetary claims it is based on a percentage of the costs. The percentages are
  • if the amount<£500,000, then 10% of the amount (so here £9,500)
  • if the amount is between £500,000 and £1 million, 10% of first £half million + 5% of the rest

Chapter 8 MOCS

The _practical_ outcome of part 36 costs is

loser pays winner EXCEPT

where offer accepted after end RP; or EXCEPT

for the period after RP where C wins less than or the same as the offer at trial.

Chapter 9

i) LIMITATION

[BSB 3; White Book Vol 2;

The Limitation Act 1980 ("LA") ss 1, 2, 32, 28(6), 28(1), 32 (1) (6),11,14, 33]

The sessions dealing with this area of the syllabus on my BPTC course are

 Activity | You may find it useful to copy the definition of Limitation Period from GL here

Under the Limitation Act 1980, it is a complete defence for D to plead that C's claim is time barred (also referred to as statute barred). C has no right to a remedy if he does not deliver the claim form to the court by the last day of the limitation period. D could then ask for strike out of the statement of case of the statute barred claim or for summary judgment in her favour in relation to it. (More on strike out and summary judgement later in chapter 16).

BSB3.1　　Rules on calculating limitation (accrual and when time stops running)

The latest time for delivering a claim form to court to be issued is no later than the last day of the limitation period.

The limitation period accrues (i.e. time starts to run)

Time starts to run

- when C ceases to be under a disability
  - minority is a disability. By **s 28 LA 1980** when C is a child at the date of the cause of action, time starts to run on their 18th birthday
  - persons suffering from mental incapacity are under a disability. Time does not run against persons under such a disability at the time of the cause of action. If this disability were brought on by the cause of action, time starts to run when C is no longer under the disability

- when fraud, deliberate concealment or mistake is the main cause of action, time starts to run only when the action is discovered, or could have been discovered with reasonable diligence. **s. 32 LA 1980. BSB 3.3** Limitation Act 1980 provisions dealing with persons under a disability, fraud, concealment and mistake

- from the date of knowledge in latent damage claims and some personal injury (PI)claims (see later in this chapter for further detail on these)

- otherwise, on the date the cause of action accrued.

The limitation period is calculated as follows.

If a cause of action accrued on Tuesday 24th of June 2014 (e.g. C ceased to be under a disability, a fraud was discovered, it is the date of knowledge in a latent damage case or a relevant PI case, a contract were breached or a negligent act occurred on that date) and there is a party capable of suing and one capable of being sued, then day one of the limitation period was Wednesday 25th June 2014.

As an example, for those causes of action whose limitation period is six years, then the last day that the claim form can be issued is 25th June 2020.

Time stops running when C delivers the claim form to court, even if it is not issued by the court on that day.

BSB 3.2   Limitation periods in tort, contract, latent damage cases, personal injuries, fatal accidents, recovery of land, judicial review and contribution claims. Also the provisions of the Limitation Act 1980, ss 14, 14A, 14B and 33;

Once time has started to run, the claim form must be issued within the following limitation periods.

- _Tort_ not causing personal injury 6 years: trespass 6 years from the date of the harmful act.

- _Contract_ 6 years from the date of the breach
  - **BSB 7.7** Remedies - applicable time limits
    - In any claim for **specific performance** of a contract of for an injunction **or for other equitable relief**, s.36 (1) Limitation Act 1980 states that for actions founded on tort or on simple contract, (and other actions not currently on the BPTC syllabus), the time limit under the Act **shall not apply except** insofar as any such time-limit **may be applied by the court by analogy.**
    - The Act goes on to say that the court may nevertheless refuse relief on the ground of acquiescence or otherwise. Case law has shown that acquiescence needs to be for many years, before relief will be refused.

- _Latent damage_ cases (e.g. in property) caused by negligence where there is no PI **s.14(A) LA 1980**
  - 6 years from accrual i.e. the date of damage as above; or
  - 3 years from the 'starting date' i.e. the earliest date C knew
    - D's identity; and
    - that the damage is sufficiently serious to justify proceedings; and
      that the damage was caused by an alleged negligence.

  - **S.14(B) LA 1980** provides a maximum of 15 years from the alleged negligent act/admission, after which latent damage cases cannot be brought.

- _Personal injury_ 3 years **s.11 LA 1980**
  - **S.14 LA 1980** Time runs from the date the cause of action accrued **or** from the date that C knew that a cause of action has accrued if that is later than the date of the cause of action itself. Time will start to run from the date C has all the following knowledge
    - that the injury is significant, plus
    - that it is attributable to the act/admission, plus
    - the identity of the defendant, plus

- o the identity of anyone with vicarious liability.

- The court has a discretion to disapply the limitation period for PI. It is recommended that you note and learn from **s.33 (3) LA 1980** what the court has regard to when deciding whether or not to disapply the time-limit for claims for personal injury or fatal accidents.

- _Fatal accidents_ 3 years **s.12 LA 1980**
  - time runs from
    - o the date of death, or
    - o the date of knowledge, of the person for whose benefit the proceedings are brought

  - **S.33 LA 1980** As above, remember the court's discretion to disapply the limitation period for fatal accidents

- _Recovery of land_ 12 years.

- _Judicial Review_ 3 months. May be extended. See the later judicial review chapter for detail on this.

- _Contribution claims_ 2 years from the relevant date which is
  - the date judgment was given, or in an arbitration when the award was given, or
  - the date a person agreed to the amount she would make in contribution

The Limitation period runs from the date of the cause of action

In PI it may run from the date of knowledge instead

In latent damage claims it runs from the date of knowledge

It runs from other dates where C is under a disability, or where the cause of action is fraud, concealment or mistake.

JR 3 months (seldom extended)

Contribution 2 years

PI/fatal accident 3 years (court can disapply)

Latent damage 3 or 6 years

Tort 6 years

Contract 6 years

Chapter 10

i) PRE-ACTION CONDUCT AND PRE-ACTION PROTOCOLS

[BSB2; White Book Section C]

The sessions dealing with this area of the syllabus on my BPTC course are	

BSB 2.1   The Practice Direction (Pre-Action Conduct)

The White Book sets out this practice direction in section III of Section C1 and annexes A and B in section IV. The idea is that

- parties aim to settle their differences without litigation
- efficient management of proceedings will be aided if proceedings do go ahead
- information is exchanged
  - C sends full details in a letter before claim to D
  - Within a reasonable period D acknowledges the letter (within 14 days), then gives a full written response within 14-30 days+ of receipt of the letter before claim, depending on the complexity of the matter
- ADR/ReDOC are considered / carried out and settlement may be reached in this way
- parties should act in a reasonable and proportionate manner

The court will ask for explanations if the parties have not complied with the practice direction.

Activity

BSB 2.3   The details of pre-action conduct where no specific protocol applies

Read sections III and IV of Section C1 of the White Book to get an idea of the detail of acceptable and required pre-action conduct. You must become conversant with this detail.

The above principles also apply to the pre-action protocols

BSB 2.2   The list of specific pre action protocols; the principles relating to pre-action conduct under the Personal Injury pre-action protocol

The list is at the very beginning of section C of the White Book. It is currently 13 items long so do become familiar with it/learn it.

Activity	Note the list of specific pre-action protocols here
	~
	~
	~
	~
	~
	~
	~
	~
	~
	~
	~
	~
	~

The Personal Injury pre-action protocol is in the fourth section of section C of the White Book. You must become conversant with this detail.

BSB 2.4   The consequences of non-compliance with pre-action protocols.

The Court expects compliance.

The Court considers the effect of a party's non-compliance on the other party.

The court may order the following sanctions

- that there is a stay (i.e. suspension) of proceedings until the relevant steps have been taken
- that there are cost consequences (e.g. the party at fault pays some or all of the other party's costs on the indemnity basis)
- that C receives no interest/lesser percentage interest on damages awarded, where C is at fault re pre-action matters but does win the action
- that D pays interest on damages awarded to C at a higher rate, where D is at fault re per-action matters

Do not go straight to litigation

Follow pre-action conduct PD

Follow pre-action protocol where there is one

There may be sanctions if you don't

Chapter 11

k) Claim Form issued and served; Particulars of Claim served

COMMENCING PROCEEDINGS [BSB4; CPR PARTS 6, 7, 8, 21]

The sessions dealing with this area of the syllabus on my BPTC course are	

The majority of the case studies on your BPTC are likely to be under the Part 7 procedure. Before dealing with those, we will look at Part 8 CPR procedure.

BSB 4.2   When the Part 8 procedure is appropriate and how Part 8 claims are commenced

The Part 8 procedure is appropriate when

- the claim is unlikely to involve any substantial dispute of fact or
- when a PD or a rule allows.

A claim under the Part 8 procedure may be made at any County Court hearing centre unless a rule, practice direction or enactment provides otherwise. However, when a claim is given a hearing date, the court may direct that proceedings should be transferred to another hearing centre if it is appropriate to do so.

One instance where Part 8 claims are therefore used is where there has been a settlement between the parties and a (potential) party to proceedings is 'under a disability', so a child or a person suffering from mental incapacity.

BSB 4.5 The procedures for **settling proceedings** by or against: children and persons suffering from mental incapacity (Part 21) The Part 8 procedure is used to give the necessary **court approval** of a settlement involving a person under a disability, otherwise the settlement is not valid. Thus these two categories of persons under a disability are prevented from settling claims at too low a value, either due to C's own disability or due to the inexperience of a lawyer.

Remember that under the CPR this means children until their 18th birthday as well as "a protected party", i.e. a person suffering from mental incapacity.

The procedure begins with a Part 8 claim form. This is in standard from which comes with comprehensive guidance on how to fill it in.

A witness statement will be filed with the claim form.

Part 8 claims are usually allocated to the multi-track (explained later in chapter 22).

Settlement hearings are heard in private, the decisions announced in public.

The court considers whether the proposed settlement is in the interest of the person under the disability (C's prospects of success balanced against the likely level of damages were D to be found fully liable if the case went to trial).

[When a settlement involving a party under a disability is reached during any Part 7 proceedings, court approval of the settlement is still needed. The procedure is then to issue an application notice with written evidence].

If the court does not approve the settlement on this occasion it is likely to adjourn the case to allow for further negotiation.

If the court does approve the settlement, it gives directions regarding how the court will administer and invest the money on behalf of the person under a disability. Where the amounts involved are large, directions will be that the money is transferred to the Court of Protection.

BSB 4.1   When the Part 7 procedure is appropriate and how Part 7 claims are commenced

The majority of the case studies on your BPTC are likely to be under the Part 7 procedure. You may wish to refer back to chapter 1 of this book to refresh your memory as to which court the type of claim you are dealing with should be started in.

Overview of how Part 7 claims are commenced

The claim form ("CF") is one of the documents known as a statement of case. It comes in standard formats and sets out the essence of the claim.

The claimant ("C") completes it and delivers it to court and the court issues it. Issue is usually the same day. The date of issue of the CF is the date stamped on the form by the court. This starts the litigation proceedings.

Remember that the CF must be delivered to the court no later than the last day of limitation period.

CF is then served, usually by the court, on the defendant ("D"). This must be done within 4 months of issue by the court.

Full details of the claim are set out either in the CF itself or in another statement of case called particulars of claim ("POC"). You will learn how to draft the POC on the BPTC. The POC can be attached to, filed with and served with the CF on D at the same time.

If the CF is issued and served on D without the POC (the POC may take some time to draft!), then the POC must be served on D within 14 days of the CF being served on her.

Detail of commencement of Part 7 claims

BSB 6.1   The requirements as to the form and content of statements of case

Where there is more than one claim that can conveniently be disposed of in the same proceedings, a single CF may be used.

How parties are named in statements of case

BSB 4.5 The procedures for bringing proceedings by or against: children and persons suffering from mental incapacity

A **child** is referred to in the heading of a statement of case as, e.g.

Miss AMY BROWN (a child, by Mr JACK BROWN her litigation friend).

A **person suffering from mental incapacity** is referred to in the heading of a statement of case as, e.g.

Mrs BRENDA GREEN (by Ms JILL SHARP her litigation friend).

An **individual** is referred to in the heading of a statement of case as, e.g. Mr KARL WHITE

BSB 4.6 The procedures for bringing proceedings by or against sole traders

A **sole trader** is referred to in the heading of a statement of case as, e.g.

Mr KARL WHITE (trading as White's laundry)

BSB 4.6 The procedures for bringing proceedings by or against partnerships, LLPs and registered companies

A **partnership** is referred to in the heading of a statement of case as, e.g.

BLACK AND WHITE (a firm);

or for LLPs:-

HART AND HIND LLP

Where D is a **Company**, include the correct designation in the heading on the statement of case. E.g. Plc, PLC, Ltd, LTD, LIMTED

BSB 4.6 The procedures for bringing proceedings by or against charities and trusts; deceased persons and bankrupts.

An unincorporated association is not a legal person. Claims will be brought by or against an individual member or members where those individuals have rights or are liable in a similar way to that in which the unincorporated association would have been, were it a legal person.

Alternatively claims could be brought by or against the committee members on behalf of themselves and all members of the unincorporated association.

For **trusts,** claims will be by or against the trustees. There is no need to join in beneficiaries. Decisions will be binding on the beneficiaries unless the court orders otherwise.

Claims survive the death of **deceased persons.** Personal representatives [(executor (male) or executrix (female) of the will, or the administrator if there is no will] can be ordered to be substituted for the deceased as parties.

Once declared **bankrupt**, a person's assets are dealt with by the trustee in bankruptcy ("TIB"). A bankrupt person is referred to in the heading of a statement of case as, e.g.

The trustee of the estate of Mr JAMES COLERIGDE, a bankrupt

A person's assets will not be dealt with by the TIB where the claim is a PI claim. The TIB must account to the bankrupt individual for general damages.

Similarly, where the claim is one for defamation the TIB will account to the defamed C for his award.

Contents of the CF

The CF must include

- the remedy C wants (if not specified, the court may still grant that unspecified remedy if it is a remedy that C is entitled to)
- a statement that the POC, if it is not being served with the CF, will follow

- **a statement of truth.** This is serious and is what gives the document its legal weight/gravitas as it verifies the factual basis of the case **BSB 6.2**

Claims for interest and costs, will be dealt with in the POC.

| Activity | Please go to PD 22.2 Note 1 in the White Book and transcribe here the wording of a **statement of truth** verifying a statement of case. |

BSB 4.3   The rules governing service of court documents within the jurisdiction

CLAIM FORM

THE RULES GOVERNING **HOW** IT IS SERVED

The CF (not a photocopy) is served on the D by the court, although can be done by C.

Use one of the **required steps**

- leave it with D (It is sufficient if C tried his hardest to do this and D is being elusive as she knows what it is)
- send it by first class post
- send it by DX (document exchange = centres where mail is exchanged using this system)
- use any other method permitted by relevant company or limited liability partnership statutes when D is a company or limited liability partnership
- Complete a facsimile (fax) transmission
- Send an email

| Activity | Please go to PD 6A in the White Book and make notes on the required detail of sending and receiving by these methods within the UK. |

THE RULES ON **WHERE** TO SERVE ON D

Where D has given the address of a solicitor

- Before doing so, you need the solicitor's indication in writing, on their headed paper that it is ok to serve it on them and by which method/step.
- Service **must** be on the solicitor

THE RULES ON **WHERE** TO SERVE ON D WHERE **D HAS GIVEN NO ADDRESS** FOR SERVICE (CPR 6.9)

<u>Children and protected parties **BSB 4.5** The procedures for bringing proceedings by or against: children and persons suffering from mental incapacity</u>

Serve on parent/guardian or, if none, the person D lives with or who takes care of her.

<u>D is an individual</u>

Serve on the individual themselves at their usual or last known address. Reasonable steps must be taken to ascertain D's current address.

<u>D is a sole trader **BSB 4.6** The procedures for bringing proceedings by or against sole traders</u>

Serve on the individual themselves at their usual or last known address. Reasonable steps must be taken to ascertain D's current address.

<u>D is a partnership **BSB 4.6** The procedures for bringing proceedings by or against partnerships, LLPs and registered companies</u>

Serve on (in no particular order)
- a partner
- a person in control at the principal place of business
- the last known place of business; you must take reasonable steps to ascertain current address

<u>D is a Company</u>

Serve on (in no particular order)
- the principal office
- the registered office
- a place with a connection to the company
- a holder of a senior position
- the last known place of business; you must take reasonable steps to ascertain current address

THE RULES ON BY **WHEN** IT MUST BE SERVED **AND WHEN** IT IS **DEEMED** TO HAVE BEEN SERVED ON D

BSB 4.4   The principles governing the validity and renewal of claim forms

CPR 7.5. By midnight on the calendar day **4 months** after issue (i.e. 4 months and a day – if issued on January 2nd, remember not to count the day itself, so day one is January 3rd and service must take place by midnight on May 3rd) otherwise the CF is no longer valid. Note that it is therefore still valid when sent in time using the required step in CPR 7.5, which is when physical service took place, even though D will be deemed to receive it after the relevant midnight. It is this latter date that will be starting point for calculating by when other steps in the proceedings must take place.

CPR 6.14. D is **deemed** to have received the CF **2 business days** after the required step in CPR 7.5.

Remember that Saturday and Sunday are not business days; remember not to count the day of the step itself.

A CF sent by the required step to the correct place

- on a Monday, will be deemed received by D (and so served on D) on Wednesday. This is because Tuesday is the first business day after Monday and the second business day is Wednesday;
- on a Friday, will be deemed received by D (and so served on D) on the following Tuesday. This is because Saturday and Sunday are not business days, the first business day after Friday is Monday and the second business day is Tuesday.

This is an **irrebuttable presumption:** even if D received the CF the next day, or if she did not receive it for several weeks, she is deemed to have received it 2 business days after the required step.

If it looks like C may be running out of time i.e. the 4 months is shortly due to expire, C can apply to court with evidence, (it will be a 'without notice' application i.e. without notice to the proposed D as D is not yet on the court record) to **extend the time limit for service** under CPR 7.6(1) and (2). Provided that the application notice is filed at court before 4 months expires, the application can still be issued or heard after the 4 month time limit. Then C can just keep on making applications to extend time further by keeping within the timeframe set out in any previous similar order that C has obtained. In this way C can get more and more time extensions (if the court will allow them). Remember that in making its decision, the court will apply the overriding objective including

- the need to enforce compliance with rules, PDs and orders
- whether there is any prejudice to the other party
- whether the date of a hearing will be affected if an extension is given.

[Full details about making without notice applications are included in the chapter entitled "interim injunctions"].

If the 4 month limit has already expired, C can still apply to court to extend the time limit under CPR 7.6 (1) and (3) for service but it will be a great hurdle he has to overcome to persuade the court to grant the order. C will need to show that

- he has acted promptly in making this application and either
- the court failed to serve the CF; or
- he has taken all reasonable steps to serve within the 4 month period but has been unable to do so.

If the court refuses the extension of time, provided the limitation period has not run out, then C can simply start afresh with a new CF.

Counsel should always be aware of how close the limitation period is to ending. Once a limitation period has ended, unless the claim is for PI or a fatal accident and the court has disapplied the limitation period, then where a CF was issued within the 4 month timeframe, but was not served, the situation cannot be rectified by simply starting afresh with a new CF.

Alternative service (by a step other than the CPR required step or at a place other than the CPR stipulated place)

If a situation arises where C has tried to ascertain D's current address / tried to serve the CF there, yet it is not proving possible to serve using the required step or on the correct the place, C may apply to court under CPR 6.15 for an order allowing **alternative service** of the CF. This will be a Part 23 application, without notice.

- application with
- evidence of good reason for needing the order
  - PD 6A paragraph 9.1 says what to deal with in your evidence if applying pre-service
  - PD 6A paragraph 9.2 says what to deal with if applying once service has been tried

- draft order (e.g. ordering that service will be effective if the CF is served on D's usual/last known address, even though it has been shown that D is no longer there).

PARTICULARS OF CLAIM ("POC")

This is a statement of case and so must contain a **statement of truth.**

THE RULES ON BY **WHEN** POC MUST BE SERVED **AND WHEN** POC IS **DEEMED** TO HAVE BEEN SERVED ON D

The POC is "a document other than a claim form" for the purposes of the CPR, here CPR 6.26. You will learn how to draft POCs during the BPTC. (Remember that in contrast, for Part 8 claims, there is simply a witness statement; no POC is used in Part 8 claims).

If ready, the POC can be served on D at the same time as the CF.

Otherwise the POC must be served on D **within 14 days of deemed service of the CF**, CPR 7.4 [and this must still be within the 4 month midnight deadline for the CF to be valid (unless there has been a disapplication of the time limit in a PI or fatal accidents case)].

Remember not to count the day of the step itself, so if the CF is deemed served 31st March, the first clear day is 1st April = day one, so the latest date for serving the POC on D is on 14th April.

For "documents other than a claim form" there are different timeframes regarding when service of such documents is deemed to have taken place. CPR 6.26.

- when the required step is sending by first class post, or in the DX, the document is deemed served on the second business day after that (the same as for a CF), whereas.
- when the required step is leaving the document with D, or completing a fax transmission, or sending an email this must be done before 4.30 to be deemed served that day, or it will be deemed served on the next business day.

C must also serve with the POC

- a response pack, plus
- if it is a PI claim (PD 16.4) a schedule of past and future losses and also medical reports. For soft tissue injury claims (whiplash) this must be a 'fixed costs medical report'.

Chapter 11 MOCS is on the next page

Part 8 when no substantial dispute of fact

Part 7

- *Issue CF within limitation period*
- *Serve CF within four months of issue*
- *CF deemed served on second business day after relevant step*
- *Serve POC within 14 days deemed serviced of CF*
- *POC deemed served re CPR 6.26*

Rules on how and where to serve

Chapter 12

I) D admits; or acknowledges service of the POC and or serves her defence

STATEMENTS OF CASE [BSB 6.3; CPR Parts 14, 10, 15, 16, 11, 12, 13]

The sessions dealing with this area of the syllabus on my BPTC course are	

Here, in diagram form is what we covered in the previous chapter regarding service of the CF and POC (w/i = within):

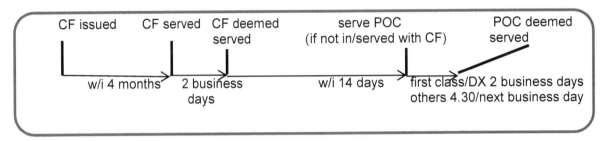

BSB 6.3 **The methods by which parties may respond to statements of case (including particulars of claim, defences, replies, counterclaims)**

RESPONDING TO PARTICULARS OF CLAIM

There are five possibilities.
- D admits everything straightaway; or
- D acknowledges the service of the POC on her; or
- D defends, drafting a statement of case called a defence and files that defence at court; or
- D may also make a claim against C in the form of a counterclaim, usually done in the same document as the defence; or
- D does nothing - neither acknowledges service on her of the POC nor responds with a defence or defence and counterclaim within the prescribed time limits.

D admits everything straightaway

This is the first possibility, the admission being **within 14 days** of deemed service of the POC. If D does not admit by then and does nothing else either, then C may apply to court for default judgment (see later in this chapter). If C for some reason does not make such an application then D can admit after the said 14 day period.

Where D has **admitted in writing** (e.g. in a notice / a statement of case / a letter), then C makes an interim **application** to court for judgement.

If the claim is simply a money claim an **admission form** can be used. C can then file a **request** at court to obtain judgement. D can request time to pay. If C and D cannot agree on this, the court can determine what should happen, e.g. D could pay by instalments.

A formal admission ends the claim and D pays fixed costs, interest and the amount of the claim.

Any informal admission will not be sufficient to allow C to apply for or request judgment.

D acknowledges service on her of the POC

This is the second possibility. D sends **AOS** to court **within 14 days** of deemed service of the POC. In it she could ask for more time to prepare her defence. If she felt it appropriate, this is where she would initiate a dispute of the court's jurisdiction.

D defends, drafting a statement of case called a defence and files that defence at court

This is the third possibility. Either
(i)   D files Defence at court **14 days** after deemed service of the POC. It is further possible for C and D to agree an extension of up to 28 days and D must notify the court of any such agreement; or
(ii)   **If D filed AOS,** D files Defence at court **28 days** after deemed service of the POC. It is further possible for C and D to agree an extension of up to 28 days and D must notify the court of any such agreement.

In diagram form - time limits for filing the defence

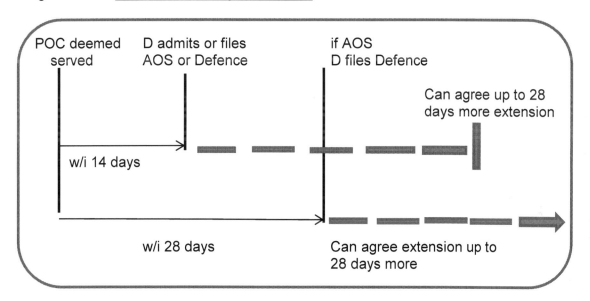

No defence needs to be filed if

– the hearing is awaited for an application by D to dispute the court's jurisdiction; or
– if the hearing is awaited for an application by C for summary judgement (see later in chapter 16 for a full explanation of summary judgment).

BSB 6.1   The requirements as to the form and content of statements of case

Form - This of the statement of case called the DEFENCE.

You will learn how to draft the form of a defence during the BPTC.

Content of the statement of case called the DEFENCE

One of the following must occur in relation to each statement in C's POC
– D requires C to prove a statement in his POC (require to prove ("**RTP**"))

- D **denies** a statement in C's POC **giving reasons why and giving her own version**
- D **admits** what C has written in his POC

- **BSB 6.3**   The effect of not responding to an allegation in a statement of case
  If D makes none of the 3 above responses to any statement in C's POC, then under CPR 16.5 she is deemed to **admit** that statement. That is **unless** in her defence document she **sets out** the nature of **her case** in relation to the issue to which that allegation is relevant, **or** unless a **money claim** is involved. In these two instances, the effect is that C is now **"RTP"** those statements.

D counterclaims against C

The fourth possibility is where D also makes a claim against C in the form of a counterclaim, usually done in the same document as the defence

This is an example of an additional claim under Part 20 CPR. Full details are in the next chapter. So if D now wants to counter with a claim against C she will include a counterclaim, usually in the same document in which she sets out her defence. The name of the statement of case will therefore include DEFENCE and COUNTERCLAIM.

RESPONDING (replying) TO A DEFENCE [AND COUNTERCLAIM]

- If D made a counterclaim, C will serve a defence to D's counterclaim. It must be filed and served within 14 days of service of the counterclaim.

- C does not have to reply to D's defence, but can do so.

  BSB 6.3   The effect of not responding to an allegation in a statement of case If C makes no response to a statement in D's defence, then C is **not taken to admit it**. If C does file a reply but fails to deal with a matter raised in the defence, then C is taken to require D to prove that statement. **"RTP".**

  C will therefore file a reply where in relation to D's defence where he wants to
  • admit something in the defence; or
  • allege facts in answer to D's defence which he had not included in his POC.

  The reply, verified by a statement of truth, must be filed at court and served on the other parties with C's directions questionnaire during the next stage of the litigation process.

- Where there is both a counterclaim and a reply, they can be included in the same document. Since the time limits for filing and serving are different, the court may order that the counterclaim and reply be filed together by the time limit as if it were a reply only. If no such order is made, the counterclaim and reply should be filed separately each within their own time limits.

D does nothing

This is the fifth possibility. D neither admits, nor acknowledges service on her of the POC nor responds with a defence or a defence and counterclaim within the prescribed time limits.

There arises here one difference between Part 7 and Part 8 claims.

For Part 8 claims, failure to acknowledge service of the CF within the required time frame means that D may not take part in the hearing unless the court gives permission. There will be no defence put forward as the parties are substantially in agreement.

For Part 7 claims, C applies for default judgement. This is one example of Judgment without trial.

<u>**BSB 13.1**</u>   <u>Default judgments, including calculating time for entry of default judgment, procedure, whether permission is required</u>

If D does not reply to the POC with an admission, an AOS or a defence within the timeframes set out in the most recent box diagram above, "time limits for filing the defence" she is in default of doing so; in default of following the CPR. That entitles C to ask for judgement without trial, which in these circumstances is known as default judgement. The box diagram shows how to calculate time for entry of default judgement.

C has until 6 months from the end of the period for D to file a defence, to apply for default judgment. If no such application is made and if no AOS or defence has been filed by then, there is an automatic stay (suspension) of proceedings [Please see later for detail on stays in the chapter 14].

There are two procedures for obtaining default judgment and the correct one must be used.

– Where the claim is for **money/value of undelivered goods** and C has filed a certificate of service of POC at court, C can **request** that default judgement is entered once the time for filing a defence has passed. No permission is required for this. Where the claim is for an unspecified amount of money, the court will decided the amount. For those County Court claims where a request for judgment which includes an amount of money to be decided by the court is filed, the claim will be sent to the preferred County Court hearing centre.

– Where the claim is for **any other remedy** than money/value of undelivered goods and C has filed a certificate of service of POC at court, C can **apply** to the court under **Part 23** CPR for default judgment.

   The outline for how to make a Part 23 application has already been set out in this book at the end of chapter 4.

Activity	Please refer back to that chapter and refresh your memory/notes on how to make a Part 23 application. You may wish to write it out again here.

When a claim includes a **mix** of a claim for money/value of goods and "any other remedy" then a **Part 23** application must be made for default judgement.

When a claim includes a mix of a claim form money/value of goods and "any other remedy" and the latter claim is abandoned, so that the remaining claim is now only for money/value of goods, then at this point C can simply request to have default judgement entered.

Costs

Remember that costs on default judgement where the claim is for specified sum > £25 = fixed costs as per part 45 Table 1. For a claim for an unspecified amount, the costs will be in the court's discretion.

Where default judgement is not available

- Claims for goods under the Consumer Credit Act
- Part 8 claims
- Where a PD says so
- Where D has made an application to get C's case struck out [Please see later in chapter 22 on strike out] and that hearing is still awaited
- Where there is an application for summary judgment [Please see later in chapter 16 on summary judgment] and that hearing is still awaited
- Where D has paid her debt to C (unless the default judgment was correctly entered, since the deemed date of service of the POC had passed and there had been no response from D within the 14 days of that deemed service, because D had not in fact received the POC. D's remedy would then be to apply to court to get the correctly entered default judgement against her set aside)
- Where a "closed material application" under the Justice and Security Act 2013 is pending [Please see later in chapter 23 in the Public Interest Immunity section].

BSB 13.1   The principles applied on applications to set aside

- D applies not more than 14 days after receiving the default judgement
- An application to set aside is a Part 23 application, to include in addition a draft of D's defence
- The court MUST set the default judgement aside if it is been wrongly entered
- The court may set it aside [or vary it] if it considers D has a real prospect of successfully defending the claim **(RPOS)** <u>or</u> if it considers that there is some other good reason to do so or to allow D to defend the claim **(SOGR)**. The court will have regard to whether the application to set aside was made **promptly.**
- [There are cases where Default Judgments have been considered to be a sanction (full details on sanctions are in chapter 22 of this book). This is not always the case as to consider them a sanction has been viewed as D needing to satisfy the criteria for both set-aside and for relief from sanctions!). If a court does consider default judgment to be a sanction, then with respect to the CPR 3.9 criteria, (see chapter 22) the court would have to be satisfied that D's delay in defaulting was not so serious a delay and that D had a good reason for the delay, as well as considering all the circumstances, including, of course, the overriding objective.]
- The likely costs order on an application to set aside is found in PD 44. in the section called "Court's discretion as to costs: rule 44.2" in the table in note 4.2; an order for "costs thrown away". This means that when a judgment is set aside, the party in whose favour the costs order is made is entitled to the costs which have been incurred as a consequence of needing to apply for the relief from the set-aside. This includes the costs of –

- preparing for and attending any hearing at which the judgment or order which has been set aside was made;
- preparing for and attending any hearing to set aside the judgment or order in question;
- preparing for and attending any hearing at which the court orders the proceedings or the part in question to be adjourned;
- any steps taken to enforce a judgment or order which has subsequently been set aside.

Chapter 12 MOCS

Please refer to the timeframes for issue and service of statements of case in the boxes in this chapter.

Default judgement for C if no response from D; request DJ is entered for money claims; Part 23 application for DJ for claims for any other remedy.

It is sometimes possible for D to get the DJ set aside if prompt application, RPOS/SOGR. Then the claim is reinstated and D gets to defend.

Chapter 13

m) PROCEEDINGS INVOLVING THREE OR MORE PARTIES AND MULTIPLE CAUSES OF ACTION

[BSB 5; CPR Part 20]

The sessions dealing with this area of the syllabus on my BPTC course are	

BSB 5.1   Multiple causes of action and multiple parties

You will learn from your BPTC that it is perfectly usual to bring more than one cause of action at one time, such as setting out a claim in both contract and the tort of negligence in relation to the same set of facts.

You will also learn that it is perfectly usual to join in more than one party, so that there can be multiple claimants and defendants in the same action.

BSB 5.2   ADDITIONAL CLAIMS

It may be that a defendant wants to add an additional claim of her own to the original main claim that C has brought against her. In so doing the defendant is aiming to pass on some or all liability to someone else.

BSB 5.3   The various types of claims that can be raised in such proceedings, and
BSB 5.4   The management of additional claims

Types of additional claim are set out in CPR 20.2 (1) (a), (b) and (c).

CPR 20.2 (1) (a)

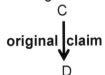

Activity

You may find it useful to copy the definition of a counterclaim
from GL here

There are two scenarios where a counterclaim can come about.

The first is where

C brings a claim against D, the original claim i.e.

C

original ‖ claim ↓

D

then D wants to counter C with a claim **against C**, i.e.

C   C

original ‖ claim   **counter ↑ claim**
↓

D   D

[It may help during the learning process to think in the following way regarding the counterclaim by D against C.

In effect, D is the claimant in the counterclaim and C is the defendant. The parties are NEVER referred to in this way, though. **The original nomenclature is always retained**].

CPR 20.4

D does not need court permission for a counterclaim against C **provided** the counterclaim is filed with her defence. That is why you will be drafting statements of case called 'Defence and Counterclaim'.

If D wishes to file the particulars of the counterclaim **at any other time, the court's permission will be needed.** The court will consider the matters set out in CPR 20.9 (2) when deciding whether or not to give permission.

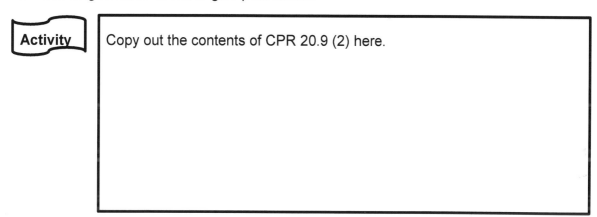

Activity | Copy out the contents of CPR 20.9 (2) here.

C puts in a defence to matters raised in the counterclaim within 14 days of deemed service of the 'Defence and Counterclaim'.

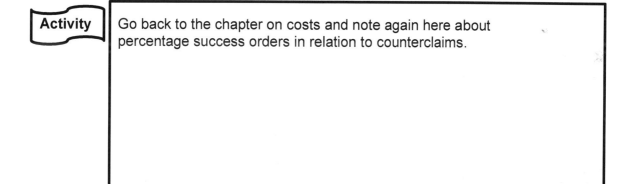

Activity | Go back to the chapter on costs and note again here about percentage success orders in relation to counterclaims.

The second is where

C brings a claim against D, the original claim i.e.

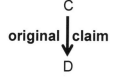
C

original | claim

D

then

D wants to counter C with a claim **against a person other than C as well as against C**,

i.e.   C   C **and a person other than C (called a Third Party (TP))**

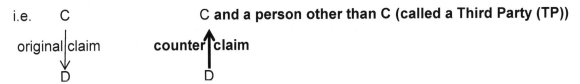

original|claim   **counter↑claim**

            ↓ |

            D   D

CPR 20.5

D needs court permission to add that other person as a party in the same proceedings.

The application can be without notice unless the court directs otherwise.

<u>CPR 20.8 (1) (a).</u> The CF for the counterclaim must be **served** on every other party (in this example, on C) **when** a copy of the **defence** to the original claim is **served**.

The court will make directions as to the management of the case.

> An additional claim by D for a contribution or indemnity against a person already a party

CPR 20.2(1)(b)

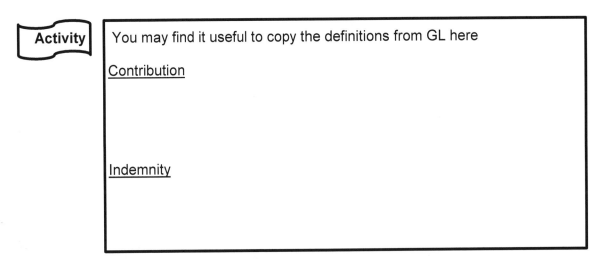

> **Activity** | You may find it useful to copy the definitions from GL here
>
> <u>Contribution</u>
>
>
> <u>Indemnity</u>

C brings a claim, **the original claim**, against two defendants, D1 and D2 i.e.

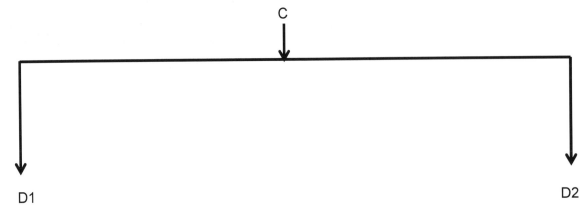

C

D1   D2

In the example here, the two Ds are already parties as C has joined them both in as Ds.

Then one of the defendants wants to claim contribution or indemnity against the other.

We will say that D1 has filed an AOS to the original claim and wants to claim contribution or indemnity against D2. (It could be the other way around).

A contribution is fault based and relates to D1's right to recover from D2 all or part of the amount that D1 is liable to pay to C.

An indemnity is D1's right to recover from D2 the whole amount which D1 is liable to pay; under contract (e.g. insurance), or by statute, or in by virtue of an agent : principal relationship.

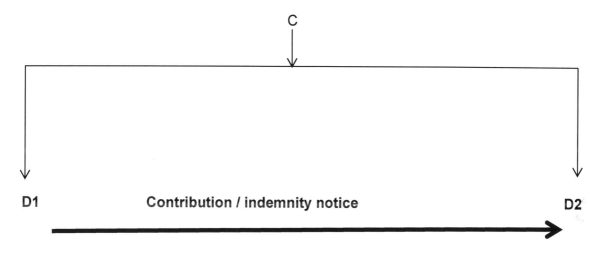

CPR 20.6

The "it" that needs to be filed and served by a D to make this type of additional claim is - CPR 20.6 (1) (a) - a notice containing a statement of the nature and grounds of her additional claim.

CPR 20.6 (2) (a) (i). **D1 does not need court permission** for an additional claim for contribution against the other D **provided** she files and serves it **with her defence** to the original claim. This can be achieved in the same statement of case.

CPR 20.6 (2) (a) (ii). Where, say, a D3 is added to the claim later and D1 or D2 wishes to claim contribution or indemnity from D3, court permission is not needed to do so if the additional claimant serves it on D3 within 28 days after D3 filed her defence.

If D1 wishes to file and serve the additional claim after she has filed and served her defence to the original claim (i.e. CPR 20 .6 (2) (b) at **any other time** than with her defence), the **court's permission will be needed**. The court will consider the matters set out in CPR 20.9 (2) when deciding whether or not to give permission.

> An additional claim by D for some other remedy than contribution or indemnity against any person not already a party.

CPR 20.2 (1) (b)

C brings a claim against D, the original claim i.e.

C

original | **claim**
↓

D

then

the additional claim is where D wants to bring a claim of her own against someone else who is not already a party, called a third party (TP).

C

original | claim
↓

D

|
| **An additional claim by D against a third party against whom C had not brought a claim in the original claim**
↓

TP

This
- saves the expense of having two trials
- safeguards against different courts providing different results on the same facts
- ensures that TP is bound by the decision regarding C and D in the original claim.

CPR 20.7, 20.8, 20.11 and 20.12

CPR 20.7 (2). D issues the CF for the additional claim against TP.

CPR 20.8 (1). Within 14 days after the date of issue of the CF,

CPR 20.7 (4). D serves CF and POC together **at the same time** on TP.

CPR 20.12. The CF and POC must be accompanied by a response pack containing

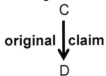

| Activity | Copy out CPR 20.12 (1) here |

CPR 20.12 (2). A copy of the additional CF must be served on every existing party (so in our example on C).

CPR 20.7 (3) (a). **D does not need court permission** for an additional claim of this type **provided** she issues the CF against TP **before or at the same time as filing her defence** to the original claim.

CPR 20.7 (3) (b) If D wishes to make the additional claim at **any other time** than before or with her defence, the **court's permission will be needed**. The court will consider the matters set out in CPR 20.9 (2) when deciding whether or not to give permission.

CPR 20.7 (5). Application for permission may be made without notice unless the court directs otherwise.

CPR 20.7 refers to CPR 15.4. So within 14 days deemed service of the {CF with POC with Response pack} on TP, TP can do one of
– Admit
– File AOS
– File Defence

CPR 20.11 (1) (b). If TP fails to file AOS or Defence, he/she is deemed to admit the additional claim and is bound by any judgment or decision in the original claim in so far as it is relevant to any matters arising in the additional claim by D against TP.

BSB 5.5   The effect on additional claims of the main proceedings being determined without trial.

Where C's original claim against D is determined without trial (i.e. where C obtains default judgment against D), then if D has satisfied the default judgment against her CPR 20.11 (3) (a) and (b), D can request judgment from the court (CPR 20.11 (2) (b)) in respect of her additional claim against TP. This judgment may be set aside or varied by the court at any time.

CPR 20.11 (3). If D has not satisfied the default judgment, she will need court permission to request judgment in respect of her additional claim against TP.

CPR 20.11 (4). The application for permission may be without notice unless the court directs otherwise.

> Where an additional claim has been made against a person who is not already a party, any additional claim made by that person against any other person (whether or not already a party.

CPR 20.2 (1) (c)

We will start with the diagram from the section above, reproduced here.

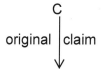

D

An additional claim by D against a third party against whom C had not brought a claim in the original claim

↓

TP

The next additional claim is where TP wants to bring a claim of his/her own against someone else who is not already a party, called a fourth party (Fourth Party).

Once the additional claim has been issued by TP against Fourth Party, then the fourth party, (who will be called by name rather than as a fourth party in statements of case), will be a party.

Once that fourth party is a party, he/she may want to bring a claim of his/her own against someone else who is not already a party, a fifth party.

Once the additional claim has been issued by the Fourth Party against the fifth party, then the fifth party, who will be called by name rather than as a fifth party in statements of case, will be a party.

And so on.

It is likely, though, that by this point, the claims should instead be made in their own right as original claims, rather than being additional to the original claim, being so far removed from it.

In diagram form

C

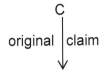

original | claim

↓

D

An additional claim by D against a third party against whom C had not brought a claim in the original claim.

↓

TP

An additional claim by TP against a Fourth Party against whom C had not brought a claim in the original claim and D had not brought a claim against in the previous additional claim.

↓

Fourth Party

CPR 20.7, 20.8, 20.11 and 20.12

The procedure each time is as previously set out under the above sub heading.

A person can add an additional claim to the main claim

as a counterclaim;

as a claim for a contribution or indemnity or as a claim for some other remedy ;

An added third party can add a claim against another person.

Chapter 14

n) If parties wish to stop proceedings for a while or to discontinue proceedings

STAYS AND DISCONTINUANCE - [BSB 16; CPR Parts 26 and 38]

The sessions dealing with this area of the syllabus on my BPTC course are	

Stays

BSB 16.3 Applications for stays [pending consent to medical examination] and the effect of stays

A **'stay'** imposes a hold on proceedings.

- Parties can **request** a stay (or the court can impose one). For example
  - where ADR/ReDOC is considered and pursued once proceedings have started; or
  - pending consent to medical examination; or
  - whilst awaiting prognosis in a PI case; or
  - where a part 36 offer has been accepted.

  The request must be made in writing at the same time as filing the directions questionnaire [Please see later in chapter 22 for more on directions questionnaires.]

  If requested by all parties the stay will be for **one month** after which it is lifted; the court will notify the parties of this.

  If the request does not come from all parties and court considers a stay is appropriate, the court will direct that the whole or part of the proceedings are stayed for one month **or for such other period as it considers appropriate.**

  Parties must tell court if a settlement is reached during the stay. Where settlement has not been reached the court can extend the stay/give such directions as it thinks appropriate.

- As set out when dealing with default judgment in chapter 12, there is an **automatic** stay imposed by the court **6 months after** the end of the period for filing the defence if
  - D has not admitted / defended / put in a counterclaim; and
  - there has been no application for default judgement or for summary judgement [Summary Judgment will be explained later in chapter 16].

  Any party can apply for an automatic stay to be **lifted** so that proceedings will continue on their way. This is a Part 23 Application. As this is a relief from a sanction, the court will consider the criteria in CPR 3.9. Full details are in chapter 22.

BSB 16.4 Discontinuing and the costs consequences of discontinuing

Discontinuing

There are times when C needs the court's permission to terminate all or part of a claim against all or any Ds and times when he does not.

He **needs permission if**

- there has been a successful interim application [We explore the various types of interim applications in chapter 16]; or
- any party has given an undertaking to the court; or
- a D who made an interim payment to C does not consent in writing to the discontinuance; or
- there are several Cs and all have not consented in writing to discontinuing the claim.

Where permission is granted discontinuance takes effect on the date set out in the order granting permission. **C files and serves a notice of discontinuance** on every party, including informing them that every party has been so served.

Otherwise, **at any time** C may terminate all or part of a claim against all or any Ds. **C files and serves a notice of discontinuance** on every party, including

- informing them that every party has been so served **and**
- providing copies of any consents given which mean that court permission for discontinuing is not needed.

Discontinuance takes effect when D is served with the notice and proceedings are brought to an end, unless within 28 days of service of this notice of discontinuance on her, D applies to have it set aside.

The costs consequences of discontinuing (this rule does not apply to the small claims track) are that unless the court orders otherwise, C pays D's costs up to and including the date of deemed service of the notice.

If the proceedings are only partly discontinued C is liable only for the costs relating to that part. Unless the court orders otherwise these costs must not be assessed until the conclusion of the rest of the proceedings.

After discontinuing a claim against D, **C can restart the proceedings** against the same D **with court permission if** D had filed a defence and the "new" proceedings are based on (substantially) the same facts as the original discontinued claim.

Parties can request a stay (lasts one month)

Automatic stay after a claim sleeps for 6 months (can be lifted)

C can effect discontinuance at any time, unless he needs permission, paying D's costs

Chapter 14 MOCS

o) AMENDING STATEMENTS OF CASE [BSB 10; CPR Part 17]

The sessions dealing with this area of the syllabus on my BPTC course are	

BSB 10.6   Costs consequences of amending

The likely costs consequence of amending statements of case is found in PD 44. in the section called "Court's discretion as to costs: rule 44.2" in the table in note 4.2 The order is likely to be for "costs of and caused by" the amendment. The amending party is usually ordered to pay the costs of the other party, unless, for example the other party unreasonably refused to consent to the amendments, thereby increasing costs.

The party in whose favour the costs order is made is entitled to the costs of preparing for and attending the application and the costs of any consequential amendments to his or her own statement of case.

BSB 10.1   Permission / consent to amend: when required, and how permission is sought;

BSB 10.2   Principles governing applications for permission to amend;

BSB 10.5   Amendments affecting accrued limitation rights

Statements of case can be amended any time before they are served.

The statements of case so far introduced in this book are the claim form ("CF"), the particulars of claim, ("POC") and the defence (and counterclaim).

A party can apply to the court for an order that any frivolous/vexatious amendments made before the statement of case is served be disallowed. The application must be made within 14 days from when the statement of case was deemed served on the applicant.

Once the CF has been served

No matter what the statement of case to be amended, the party wishing to amend must apply to the **court** for **permission** to do so.

AMENDING STATEMENTS OF CASE *BEFORE* THE END OF THE RELEVANT LIMITATION PERIOD

Where the amendment is to add / substitute / remove a party (there can be any number of Cs or Ds).

Adding a party

An existing party or a person who wishes to be added as a party may make the application. The applicant needs
– the written consent of HMRC if that is whom they wish to add as a party
– the written consent of any party to be added as a claimant
– to file that consent at court with the application notice for court permission.

The court is likely to grant the order if
– it is desirable to add the additional party so that the court can resolve the case; or

- there is an issue involving the new party (Y) and the existing party (X) connected to the case and the addition of the new party is desirable so that the court can resolve the case.

Substituting a party

An existing party or a person who wishes to be substituted as a party may make the application.

The applicant needs
- the written consent of HMRC if that is whom they wish to add as a party
- the written consent of any party to be substituted as a claimant
- to file that consent at court with the application notice for court permission.

The court is likely to grant the order if
- the substitution is because the existing party's interest or liability has passed to Y because either X has died and Y is his executor, or because X is bankrupt and Y is his trustee in bankruptcy; **and**
- it is desirable to substitute Y for X so that the court can resolve the case.

Removing a party

The court can order that a party be removed if it considers it is not desirable that they are a party.

Once an order has been given to add, substitute or remove a party from a statement of case

The order must be served on all parties and on any other person that the order affects.

The court may give consequential directions regarding filing and serving documents and the management of the case.

Where the amendment is for **something other** than to add / substitute / remove a party

On applying for court permission, the person wishing to amend needs
- the written consent of the other parties
- to file the consent at court.

If all the parties do not consent in writing the court may nevertheless grant permission.

AMENDING STATEMENTS OF CASE *AFTER* THE END OF THE RELEVANT LIMITATION PERIOD

This could occur, for example, where the cause of action in contract accrued over 6 years ago and the claim form was issued in time, but it has taken a long time to progress through the litigation process and the six-year limitation period has now passed.

BSB 10.3   Introducing new causes of action

Where, for example, a claimant wishes to amend the statement of case, to add negligence to or substitute negligence for the contract claim, or to add in a counterclaim or a set-off, when applying for court permission he must show that the new claim arises out of (substantially) the same facts for which he has already claimed a remedy. In exercising its discretion the court will consider the promptness of the application and the prospects of success of the new claim.

<u>Correcting a mistake in a name.</u>

For example changing Catherine to Kathryn.

The mistake must be
- as to the name and not one that would cause reasonable doubt as to the identity (e.g. the right description, the wrong name)
- genuine
- such that no-one was misled.

BSB 10.4   Adding or substituting parties

Proceedings must have started during the limitation period and adding/substituting must be **necessary** in one of the following three ways in order to progress the case to its conclusion.

- Y was the intended party and X was there in mistake for Y; i.e. the wrong entity was used, e.g. another company with a similar name, another John Smith and so the mistake can only be cured by this substitution.

- The new Y needs to be substituted or added for the claim to be properly carried on by or against the original X.

- X dies so X's executor needs to be substituted; X is bankrupt so X's trustee in bankruptcy needs to be substituted.

To amend a statement of case once the CF has been served, court permission is needed.

Otherwise amendment before service of statement of case does not need court permission.

File written consents with application notice for permission

Written consent is necessary for adding or substituting a claimant

After the limitation period, introducing a new cause of action must arise from (substantially) same facts

After the limitation period, amending the name of the same party must arise from genuine non-misleading mistake

After the limitation period adding or substituting a party must be necessary as set out in the CPR.

Chapter 16

"What if" (i)

STRIKING OUT; JUDGMENT WITHOUT TRIAL

[BSB 16, CPR PART 3; BSB 13, CPR PART 24; BSB 27]

The sessions dealing with this area of the syllabus on my BPTC course are	

In this book you have already been introduced to applications under part 23 CPR, in the chapter on disclosure before proceedings and again in the chapter on statements of case in the section on default judgement.

Applications under **Part 23 CPR** are often referred to as interim applications because they are made in the interim stages of the litigation process, either before proceedings are issued or between proceedings commencing and trial.

If a claim were procedurally straightforward, then once a defence has been filed the next stage of the process would be the court giving notice to the parties of the proposed track allocation.

The completion and filing of parties' directions questionnaires follows this. Where a party wishes to apply for interim remedies - in this chapter strikeout or summary judgement - their intention to do so should be included with their directions questionnaires when they are filed at court.

Before continuing on in this book to look at track allocation and beyond, we are now first going to pause to consider the interim applications and remedies that parties may seek on the way to trial - those that may arise at the defence stage and afterwards. This section of the book is therefore called the "what if" section- "What if one of the following circumstances arises at or after the defence stage?"

WHAT IF D THINKS THERE ARE NO REASONABLE GROUNDS FOR BRINGING THE CLAIM?

D could choose to apply for
- the remedy of strike out; and / or
- summary judgment.

BSB 16.1   Identification of whether, in any given case, an application should be made for [sanctions or to] strike out

BSB 16.2   The procedure for applying [for sanctions], to strike out [and for relief from sanctions], and the principles applied by the court

D can apply for strikeout after AOS/Defence

- If C's statement of case shows no reasonable grounds for bringing the claim; or
- If the claim would be an abuse of court process likely to obstruct the just disposal of proceedings (because it is vexatious, scurrilous or obviously ill founded); or
- if there has been a failure to comply with a rule, PD or court order

then the court will order written material to be deleted from a statement of case so that it may not be relied upon and the court may then make any consequential order.

Note that although dealt with here in the context of D applying to strike out, this CPR rule can be used in relation to any statement of case and is framed so that for example **C could ask for D's defence to be struck out**

- if the defence shows no reasonable grounds for defending the claim; (if the claim is a money claim only, for more than £25 then a strike out on this ground incurs fixed costs as per Table 1 in Part 45 CPR; or.
- if the defence would be an abuse of court process, likely to obstruct the just disposal of proceedings (because it is vexatious, scurrilous or obviously ill founded); or
- if there has been a failure to comply with a rule, PD or court order

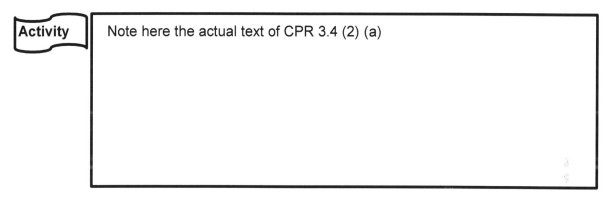

Activity Note here the actual text of CPR 3.4 (2) (a)

Yet beware when answering assessment SAQs that you need to be conscious not to simply 'learn and churn' the CPR rule. The best answers will also apply the CPR rule to the facts in the given scenario.

So remember to **apply the CPR**.

"If D can persuade the court that C's particulars of claim shows no reasonable grounds for bringing the claim, then the court may order a strike out of the claimant's particulars of claim."

"If C can persuade the court that D's defence shows no reasonable grounds for defending the claim, then the court may order a strike out of the defence."

BSB 27.10   Previous judgments, comprising res judicata, abuse of process

Res judicata translates as 'the thing has already been adjudicated'.

If C seeks to reopen old litigation/renew an issue, i.e. with the same parties, facts and cause of action which has already been finally adjudicated, the court may strike out this attempt at proceedings as an abuse of process, where either the court's findings or a compromise in the previous action estop C from bringing fresh proceedings.

Summary Judgment

BSB 13.2   Summary judgments, including the procedure, who may apply, the test
                to be applied

Summary judgement is the second way of obtaining **judgement without trial.** (Remember that we have also seen default judgment, that is obtaining judgement against D in default of D filing AOS/defence as set out in the chapter called "statements of case").

The test to be applied

A party may apply for summary judgment where that party (the applicant) considers that the other (the respondent), in respect of the claim or on a particular issue has

No real (i.e. not fanciful, imaginary or false) **prospect of succeeding in the claim/successfully defending the claim AND** there is
No other compelling reason (no witnesses or experts to enhance a party's case) **for** the case/issue to be disposed of at **trial**

Who may apply

D can apply for summary judgment at any time once proceedings have been commenced.

C can apply after he has seen D's AOS/Defence; C can apply before that if the court gives permission or if a PD so provides; if C applies before the defence is filed, D need not file a defence before the summary judgment hearing.

C cannot apply for summary judgement in relation to a D's home, nor in an Admiralty claims *in rem* e.g. seizing a vessel.

Any party who is in the position of a C or a D may apply for summary judgment. Remember that in a counterclaim where D is counterclaiming against C, D is still called D in the statements of case, although she is in the position of a C with respect to the counterclaim. C is still called C in the statements of case, although he is in the position of a D with respect to the counterclaim.

As usual, under CPR 3.3 **the court** could exercise its powers to make an order, (here for summary judgment) **of its own initiative**, rather than on an application.

Awarding summary judgement is not in contravention of Article 6 ECHR, the right to a fair trial.

The procedure

This is a Part 23 application with some slight differences to the way we have met it before.

Whereas the rule for other interim applications is to serve the application notice at least 3 clear days before the court is to deal with the application at the interim application hearing.....

..... for Summary Judgment, once the applicant has the hearing date set by the court

- A serves the notice on R at least **14 clear days** before the hearing
- R serves on A written Evidence in Response at least **7 clear days** before the hearing
- A serves on R written Evidence in Reply at least **3 clear days** before the hearing.

Both parties file & serve a statement of costs 24 hours before hearing.

Unless the court orders otherwise, copies must be served on every other party.

Written evidence need not be filed again if it was previously filed with the original claim.

<u>After the judgment</u>

Fixed costs as per Part 45 CPR Tables 1 and 4.

Where an application for summary judgment is unsuccessful, it is open to the applicant to appeal that decision. [A chapter on appeals appears later in this book].

BSB 13.2 **How the test applies where there are counterclaims and set-offs**

<u>Counterclaims</u>

Please refresh your memory on counterclaims from chapter 13.

Although summary judgement can be claimed on all or part of a counterclaim, it may not be claimed if there is a set-off situation.

<u>Set-offs</u>

In layman's terms, if I owe you £15 and you owe me £20, you should pay me £5. Setting off what I owe you against what you owe me results in you paying me £5.

In legal terminology, a set-off operates as a defence. You will learn in the drafting course on the BPTC to state the set-off at the end of a defence when there is a set-off situation. You will also learn that a D claims the amount of the set-off in her counterclaim against C. (D owes C £15 and C brings a claim against D for that £15; at the end of D's defence she states that there is a set-off situation in that C owes her £20; D therefore counterclaims against C, claiming the £5 that he owes her.)

Such mutual debts for liquidated (definite) amounts, (there is no need for the debts to be connected), is one situation where a set-off may occur.

Further situations where set-offs may occur (and so summary judgment cannot be claimed) are where

– C claims the unpaid price on a contract for the **sale of goods**; D can set off against this her counterclaim for C's **breach of statutory duty** – perhaps D's defence is that the goods were not of satisfactory quality, which is why D has not paid any or all of the price
– C is a workman claiming payment for **services**; D can set off against this her counterclaim that the standard of workmanship was **poor**
– C is a landlord claiming for **rent arrears**; D can set off against this her counterclaim that the landlord is in **breach of covenants in the lease arise**
– An equitable set-off is claimed – where if none of the above situations arise, it would nevertheless be inequitable not to set off D's defence and counterclaim against C's claim.

Thus if a counterclaim amounts to a set-off where the amount set off in D's defence (£20) is equal to or greater than the value of the claim (£15), there is a real prospect of successfully defending the claim and C cannot apply successfully for summary judgement.

Whereas on a counterclaim amounting to a set-off where the amount set-off (say £7000) is **less** than the claim (say £15,000), **C can claim summary judgement** for the undisputed £8,000 balance as there is a real prospect of succeeding in the claim.

BSB 13.2   The cheque rule, conditional orders

The cheque rule

Set-off is not available in an action on a dishonoured cheque. There is no defence to a dishonoured cheque. Summary judgement is thus available.

Therefore where there is an underlying contract to buy goods and a collateral contract to pay for them by cheque, C should sue on the collateral cheque contract, not on the contract for the sale of goods.

Let's say that C sells a car to D and that D pays £15,000 for it by cheque.
D then has to spend £7,000 on the car in repairs, and so stops the £15,000 cheque.

If C claims on the contract for the sale of the car, D can raise the repairs as a defence and set-off the £7,000 she paid for the repairs. C could claim summary judgment for the undisputed £8,000.

Whereas, if C claims on the collateral cheque contract, D can only raise defences relating to the cheque itself. With no defence to a dishonoured cheque and set-off not available to D, C can claim summary judgment for the full £15,000.

Conditional orders

Where a court thinks a respondent's case possible but improbable, the court makes a conditional order. This means that the case carries on with certain conditions. The respondent has to pay a sum of money into court and/or take a specified step i.e. the respondent has to "put their money where their mouth is". If (s)he doesn't comply then the claim will be dismissed or her/his statement of case struck out.

Chapter 16 MOCS

Apply to <u>strike out</u> all or part of a statement of case

if the other side shows no reasonable grounds for bringing or defending; or

if abuse of process

and / or apply for <u>Summary Judgement</u> NRPOS <u>AND</u> NOCR.

Chapter 17

"What if" (ii)

FURTHER INFORMATION [BSB 11, CPR Part 18, PD 18]

The sessions dealing with this area of the syllabus on my BPTC course are

BSB 11.1   When it may be appropriate to make a request for further information

What if D needs more information when she sees papers (not only statements of case) from C [or if any party needs more information when seeing the papers of another]?

D as the first party would **request further information** from C as the second party where matters are not clear / precise. Or the court may of its own initiative at any time order clarification / a party to give additional information.

BSB 11.2   The principles on which requests for further information may be administered or are allowed

Such requests are not usually used on the small claims track, although they can be.

The first party sends a written request for further information to the second party
- in a single comprehensive document containing only the request
- keeping it to what is reasonably necessary for preparing the case/understanding the other side's case
- keeping it proportionate
- by email if possible
- stating the date and allowing a reasonable time for a response

BSB 11.3   How to respond to a request for further information.

File at court the written response, verified by a statement of truth, signed by the second party / their legal representative and serve it on the other parties.

If the second party cannot or will not respond, e.g. where they are claiming that the information is privileged, or that the cost of procuring the information would be disproportionate in the circumstances, then that second party must promptly inform the other in writing of the reasons for the lack of response.

If there is no response, the first party applies under Part 23 for a court order that further information be provided; so

- **application notice** (there is no need to serve this on the non-responsive second party; it must be served on a second party who did respond and on all other parties)
- **written evidence** re the above, including details of any response
- **draft order** remembering to include costs.

The court can deal with the request without a hearing if 14 days have passed since the reasonable time for response stated in the first party's written request.

Costs

These may be summarily assessed.

Parties can request further information from each other.

The request is made to the other party in writing including a statement of truth; if no information is received in response, apply to court.

Chapter 18

"What if" (iii)

SECURITY FOR COSTS

[BSB 17, CPR Part 25]

The sessions dealing with this area of the syllabus on my BPTC course are	

What if D has concerns that C will not be able to afford to pay D's costs when/if D wins?

The same question arises when there is a party in the position of a D. We have met before the C who is in the position of a D when D has counterclaimed against C. There are other such situations

- where D lost at trial and appeals to a higher court (D is now the appellant) and has concerns that C (now the respondent) will not be able to afford to pay D's costs when/if D wins; or then
- where D wins that appeal and so C appeals (C is now the respondent who also appeals) the higher court decision and C has concerns that D will not be able to afford to pay C's costs when/if C wins.

The answer is that the party in the position of a D makes an application for an order for security for costs; an order whereby that D obtains some comfort that C is good for the payment of costs, shown by C giving some security for it.

C may be ordered to give this security by paying some money into court or by obtaining and giving a guarantee for the costs or by providing some other security. **BSB 17.7** <u>The Court's power to make orders subject to conditions.</u> The conditions arising out of the order will be that proceedings will be stayed until that condition has been fulfilled. If C does not provide the security, D can apply to have the claim struck out. (Please refer to chapter 22 for more on strike out).

BSB 17.4   Procedure on applications for security for costs

D can make the Part 23 application after serving her AOS/defence. It may be made at any stage of the proceedings after that, but should be made promptly as soon as the facts justifying the order are known.

BSB 17.6   The approach to the discretion to order security for costs in these cases

The court **will** make such an order **if** in all the circumstances (remember the overriding objective and the need for things to be just and proportionate)
- it is **JUST** to do so (balancing the possible prejudice to the parties)
- **AND**
  - An Enactment so provides or
  - **ONE** CPR 25.13 (2) condition **BSB 17.7** exists
    - **BSB17.5** C is resident outside the jurisdiction (mostly for when C is resident in the extended world beyond Europe)
    - **BSB17.5** C is an impecunious company; C is a company in or outside GB and there is reason to believe that C **will be unable** to pay D's costs. The court in exercising its discretion may include in its considerations of all the circumstances e.g. whether
      - C's claim is bona fide
      - C has reasonable prospects of success
      - D has admitted anything

- The proposed payment into court or any open offer is substantial
- D's application is to stifle a genuine claim
- C's want of means was caused by D's conduct or breach
- D's application is late in the proceedings

○ C, to evade proceedings, has changed address since the claim started
○ C gave no or an incorrect address on the claim form
○ C is acting as a nominal claimant (this condition does not refer to party or group actions)
○ C has taken steps with his assets which would make it difficult to enforce a costs order against him.

Chapter 18 MOCS

D may make a Part 23 application for security for costs.

Order made if

in all circumstances, to do so is

just and

C resides in the extended world beyond Europe; or

C is an impecunious company; or

another CPR 25.13 (2) condition exists; or an enactment so provides.

Chapter 19

"What if" (iv)

INTERIM PAYMENTS

[BSB 17, CPR Part 25]

The sessions dealing with this area of the syllabus on my BPTC course are	

Underlined heading: What if C wants to claim an advance payment of what he believes he will win in damages?

C applies for an interim payment; a payment to C from D on account of damages.

C can apply after the end of the period for D filing the AOS and may make more than one application for an interim payment.

BSB 17.2   Grounds for applying for interim payments, to include cases with more than one defendant

The court may make an order where any of the following are satisfied

- D has admitted liability to pay
- C already has judgement, with damages yet to be assessed
- The court is satisfied that if the claim went to trial, C **would** obtain judgement against D (i.e. D would be found liable) for a **substantial amount** ("amount" is known as quantum) against that D, whether or not that D is the only D or one of a number of D's
- C wants an order for possession of land and the court is satisfied that if the case went to trial, D would be liable to pay a sum of money for her occupation and use of the land whilst this claim was pending (even if the claim for possession against her fails)
- Where there are 2 or more Ds and an order for interim payment is sought against one or more of them and
  - the court is satisfied that if the matter proceeds to trial, C would obtain judgement for a substantial amount of money against at least one of the Ds (but the court cannot determine which) **and**
  - all the defendants are either
    - insured; or
    - the motor insurance bureau will meet the liability; or
    - the defendant is a public body.

Unless D agrees, an interim payment is not disclosed to the trial judge until all questions of liability and quantum have been decided.

BSB 17.3   Amount to be ordered by way of interim payment, including the effect of set-offs and counterclaims

The court should order that not more than a reasonable proportion of the likely amount of the final judgement should be made as an interim payment.

The court must take into account when ordering the amount of any interim payment, any contributory negligence by C and any relevant set-off or counterclaim by D.

BSB 17.1   The principles and procedure relating to applications for interim payments

This is a Part 23 application but with the same slight differences (as for summary judgement) that we mentioned before.

Activity You may wish to refer back to chapter 16 and the procedure on summary judgement and copy out those timeframes again here.

The evidence supporting an application for an interim payment of damages is set out in 25BPD.2. Evidence

- the amount sought
- the items regarding which it is sought
- the likely amounts on final judgement
- the reasons for believing that one of the grounds for applying is satisfied
- any other relevant matters
- if PI, details of special damages and past and future loss
- if a fatal accident, details of the person on whose behalf the claim is made and the nature of the claim; and
- exhibit any documents in support including medical reports.

<u>In a final judgement</u>

Where an interim payment has previously been made, adjustments will be made to reflect that. If the interim payment was more than the total amount awarded by the judge an order should be made for repayment, reimbursement, variation or discharge and for interest on the overpayment.

Chapter 19 MOCS

Once the period for filing AOS is over, C can apply for an interim payment if one of the grounds is satisfied.

Final judgement will make appropriate adjustments

Chapter 20

"What if" (v)

INTERIM INJUNCTIONS ("II")

[BSB 18, CPR Part 25; 25 APD; CPR 81; CPR volume 2 section 15; BSB 12]

The sessions dealing with this area of the syllabus on my BPTC course are	

What if the claimant wants an injunction either to stop the defendant doing something or to require the defendant do something?

When C wants to prohibit D from acting in violation of C's legal rights (i.e. when C wants to stop D from doing something), C applies for a prohibitory injunction.

When C wants to require D to do something, C applies for a mandatory injunction.

An injunction is an equitable remedy and so it must appear **just and convenient** to the court to grant it. The applicant must have a **substantive cause of action**.

Although final injunctions may be granted at the trial for the substantive cause of action, in this chapter we are talking about interim injunctions. These are injunctions applied for "in the interim," at a hearing somewhere along the way to the trial. The party applying for the interim injunction is called the applicant, the other party, the respondent.

BSB 18.1   The procedure for applying for an interim injunction

Prohibitory Injunctions

First, please refer back to the previous chapter in this book called "Interim Injunctions (I)". You should recall that it is possible to apply for an interim injunction before proceedings have been issued as well as after they have been issued.

Procedure

The procedure is broadly the same, whether proceedings have been issued or not. If proceedings have not been issued when an urgent prohibitory injunction is needed, the applicant will have to undertake (i.e. make a solemn and binding promise) to issue proceedings.

When proceedings - that is the CF - have been issued before an urgent prohibitory injunction is needed, there is obviously no need to undertake to issue them! Where the CF has already be issued and the application for an interim injunction is nevertheless urgent, the application may still be made without notice.

The procedure is an application under Part 23. For the purposes of this book the procedure for making a Part 23 application has been transcribed from the end of chapter 4 (application notice – written evidence – draft order) into this chapter and then **amended in bold** as appropriate to show the **additional** procedure for **urgent prohibitory injunctions.**

- Issue claim form **(if time). If there was no time to issue the CF, unless the court orders otherwise, there will be an order at the hearing for A to undertake to issue the CF immediately; or the court will give directions for the commencement of the substantive claim.**

- APPLICATION NOTICE to be issued **(if time)**
  - Complete it and get it issued at the court where proceedings in this matter are likely to be started unless there is good reason to apply to different court. **If there was time to issue the application notice, file it + evidence + draft order at court 2hrs before the hearing.**

  - State the <u>order sought and why it is sought.</u> [When answering the SAQs remember to actually state the name of the order sought and why you need it in relation to the scenario about which you are answering the question; <u>applying</u> learned elements of the CPR in your answers is a good thing]. The notice will state the date, time and place of the hearing.

- Remember that the application notice need not be served on the respondent (and so would be a 'without notice' application) if
  - there is exceptional urgency. If the urgency renders it impossible to serve the application notice on the respondent giving the usual 3 clear days' notice for a Part 23 application, the applicant must still notify the respondent informally. **The applicant must provide the draft order at the hearing and undertake to file / serve the application notice and the evidence in support on the same or next working day or as ordered by the court;** or if
  - the overriding objective is furthered by not doing so; or if
  - all parties consent; or if
  - a court order, rule or PD so allows.

- EVIDENCE
  - include *written evidence* with the application notice
  - include all material facts
  - evidence can be in the application notice itself if it is verified by a statement of truth
  - evidence can be in a statement of case verified by a statement of truth
  - evidence is often a witness statement [including exhibits] verified by a statement of truth
  - **show why there was no time to issue the claim form**
  - **show why it is a without notice application**
  - **state what informal notice has been given to the respondent**
  - **BSB 12.4** <u>Duty of full and frank disclosure in without notice applications</u>. **As the court is wholly reliant on the information provided by A,**
    - **A has a duty to investigate the facts and to present fairly the evidence on which he relies**
    - **A must disclose fully all matters relevant to the application including all matters, whether of fact or law, which are, or maybe, adverse to his application**
    - **if A is proven not to have made full and frank disclosure the order made for an interim injunction may be discharged.**

- A DRAFT OF THE REQUESTED ORDER
  - attach it to the application notice
  - **if without notice, state the return date for a further hearing at which the other party can be present**
  - **include a statement of R's right to apply to set aside or vary the order within 7 days of its service**
  - **set out clearly what R is prohibited from doing following a successful application**

- A will give undertakings (mostly to do what they have not had time to do!) The interim injunction will be discharged if A fails to comply with the undertakings in the order or if there had been a material nondisclosure by A. E.g. Undertakings to
  - issue the claim form immediately
  - pay the CF issue fee the same / next working day
  - file / pay the application notice fee the same / next working day
  - serve the application notice as soon as practicable
  - file and serve evidence as soon as practicable
  - serve the interim order as soon as practicable
  - pay any damages which R sustains and which the court considers that A should pay
- CPR 81.9 and PD 81 - include a penal notice BSB 23.4 Penal notices in interim injunction orders [Service will be by personal service so that the penal notice can be enforced by committal. The effect of non-compliance with the terms of an order amounts to contempt. The standard of proof is the criminal one, Beyond Reasonable Doubt. Contempt is punishable by fine – prison - sequestration. Application for committal can be to any single Judge of the High Court.
- include a skeleton argument
- take a copy of the draft order to the hearing on a disk/digital stick.

The hearing can be by telephone.

After the hearing, where an urgent pre-action interim injunction is ordered, serve the CF and unserved application notice with the order for the injunction where possible.

BSB 18.2 American Cyanamid principles (American Cyanamid Co v Ethicon Ltd BSB[1975] AC 396)

This provides guidelines/principles for a court to follow when exercising its **discretion** as to whether or not to allow an application for an interim injunction, so that it is not necessary to consider all the evidence regarding the merits of the case at the interim application stage.

As mandatory interim injunctions are one of the variations to American Cyanamid, it follows that the American Cyanamid principles apply to **interim prohibitory injunctions.**

The principles that Counsel should argue to persuade a court to grant an interim prohibitory injunction, to prohibit acts in violation of the claimant applicant's legal rights are, **in this order**

- That there is a **serious issue to be tried.** If yes, continue on to argue the next point. The court will refuse the injunction if there is not a serious issue to be tried.

- **Would damages be an adequate remedy for A** (i.e. would money suffice rather than an injunction)? If so, the court will refuse the injunction as an injunction would therefore not be needed. Damages would not be an adequate remedy in the following circumstances; where
  - R is unlikely to be able to pay the sum of damages likely to be awarded against her at trial; or
  - the damage is irreparable; or
  - the damage is not translatable into money terms e.g. a libel / nuisance claim; or
  - there is no available market elsewhere to buy items that would be the subject of the injunction ; or
  - damages are difficult to assess; or

- there is a provision in a contract for liquidated damages for a sum lower than A could be awarded on a successful claim for breach of the contract.

Once Counsel has established that damages would not be an adequate remedy for A, continue on to argue the next point.

- **Would A's undertaking in damages provide adequate protection for R?** (This particular principle of *American Cyanamid* can be dispensed with where the claimant/applicant is publicly funded).

The court considers how it would be if A undertook to pay compensation to R if the interim injunction is granted against R and if it ultimately turns out that the interim injunction was wrongly granted; would R is adequately protected by being awarded compensation from A in these circumstances? Once Counsel has advocated in order to persuade the court that R would thus be adequately compensated for any loss caused by the interim injunction, then Counsel should go on to argue the next point.

- Where does **the balance of convenience** lie? This principle suggests that if it lies in favour of neither one party nor the other, then the "status quo" should prevail and no interim injunction should be granted where positions are "evenly balanced."

"Status quo" is either
- the position as it was immediately before the issue of the claim form claiming the permanent injunction; or,
- if there has been unreasonable delay between the issue of the claim form and the application for the interim injunction, the position as it was immediately before this interim application.

- Counsel can also ask the court to consider any **special factors**.

- Counsel will only argue and the court will only consider the **merits of the case** as a **last resort** if the strength of one party's case is disproportionate to that of the other.

As you would expect, the principles that Counsel should argue to persuade a court NOT to grant an interim prohibitory injunction are the converse of the above, as well as showing the existence any of the usual bars to equitable remedies such as delay or no clean hands.

BSB 18.5   The meaning and effect of the usual undertakings and cross undertakings given in interim injunction cases.

Undertakings

An undertaking is a solemn binding legal promise. We have already seen the undertaking that A will give in the American Cyanamid principles, where A undertakes to pay damages to R if it turns out that the interim injunction was wrongly granted; and that this undertaking must be adequate protection for R should that turn out to be the case.

We have also seen undertakings by A to do what he has not already done in urgent interim injunctions and how a penal notice is included in an order for an urgent interim injunction so that breach of the undertaking included in the order amounts to contempt of court.

Cross undertakings *the same as*

R may choose not to contest an application for an interim injunction. In this case R gives undertakings to A ~~akin~~ to what A wanted in the injunction. R will be in contempt if she breaches these undertakings.

A must give a cross undertaking in damages to protect R so that she will receive compensation from A in the event that at trial A is not granted a final injunction.

BSB 18.3 **The principles governing the following EXCEPTIONS AND VARIATIONS to American Cyanamid:**
applications for mandatory interim injunctions, interim injunctions that finally dispose of the case, cases where there is no arguable defence, restraint of trade cases, defamation claims and cases involving freedom of expression and privacy;
BSB 18.4 **How those principles apply in the particular circumstances.**

There follow some exceptions and variations to the use of the American Cyanamid principles.

– Cases where there is no arguable defence

Where this is the case, the court will not consider the balance of convenience. An interim injunction will be granted subject to the usual equitable considerations.

Remember that where the requirements for a successful application for summary judgment are met, it is possible to apply for summary judgement including a final order for an injunction rather than just applying for an interim injunction.

– Interim injunctions that finally dispose of the case

A successful interim application will be a final disposal of the case at the interim stage where Counsel persuades the court that overwhelmingly on the merits of the case, if the interim injunction is granted there is no realistic possibility either
  • of R insisting on continuing on to trial; or
  • of the claim proceeding to trial.

– Restraint of trade cases

It may be that a contract of employment contains restraint of trade clauses to protect the employer. For example, it may provide that after an employee leaves the employ of that employer, the employee may not, for a period of, say, six months, work for a competitor, or may not work in the same line of business in the same town.

Where trial cannot be arranged before a restrictive covenant comes to an end, (i.e. say the court date is 8 months hence and the restrictive covenants were for 6 months), an interim injunction will protect the contractual rights of the employer.

Courts **will** grant an interim injunction in favour of the employer if

1 • all the facts are before the court; and
2 • the covenants in restraint of trade are prima facie valid (reasonable in time, place and activity they restrain).

If there is any doubt about no. 2, court applies American cyanamid

- Defamation claims

The overriding public interest is in the right to free speech.

Where an applicant is bringing a claim for slander or libel, there will be **no injunction** to stop the respondent from saying or writing what the applicant considers defamatory where the respondent is pleading the defence that the imputation conveyed by the statement complained of is **substantially true** and the alleged defamation is not obviously untruthful.

- Cases involving freedom of expression

Subject to a restriction for the protection of the reputation and rights of others [Art 10 (2) ECHR], everyone has the right to freedom of expression [Art 10 (1) ECHR].

So where the applicant wishes to obtain an in interim injunction to stop the respondent publishing something [s.12 (3) HRA 1998], Counsel will have to satisfy the court that at trial the applicant is likely to establish, on the balance of probabilities, that his Art 10 (2) reputation and rights justify being protected.

- Cases involving privacy

Where the applicant wishes to obtain an interim injunction to stop, say, a newspaper or magazine publishing an article or photographs, he is claiming his Article 8 (1) ECHR right to protection of private and family life.

The court will balance that right against the rights of the respondent to her Article 10 (1) ECHR freedom of expression.

The court is likely to grant the interim injunction where it is satisfied that on the balance of probabilities the applicant is likely to establish a breach of his privacy as there has been a breach of confidence. In such cases, restricting the respondent's Article 10 right to freedom of expression is justified.

Where there has been no breach of confidence the court will consider whether there is any public interest served by not granting an interim injunction, thus allowing the information about the applicant's private or family life to be disclosed.

- Mandatory interim injunction [CPR volume 2 section 15]

This is where the applicant is asking the court to make an order that the respondent do something, e.g. effect repairs. In such interim applications there is a variation to the way that the American Cyanamid principles are applied. At the balance of convenience stage Counsel needs to persuade the court that it can have **a high degree of assurance** that at the trial it would appear that the mandatory injunction was rightly granted at the interim stage, given the merits of the claimant's cause of action.

The overriding consideration is to **keep the risk of injustice as low as possible**, either
- in case it turns out at trial that the applicant wins and so a mandatory interim injunction should have been granted where it was not; or
- in case it turns out that a mandatory interim injunction should not have been granted as the applicant continues on to fail at trial. Granting a mandatory interim injunction gives a greater risk of injustice and to persuade the court to grant one, Counsel will have to show that there is more risk of injustice if it is not granted than if it is.

Chapter 20 MOCS

Procedure for urgent without notice interim injunctions

American Cyanamid principles for interim prohibitory injunctions

Exceptions and variations to the use of those principles in certain applications for prohibitory injunctions.

Mandatory interim injunctions

BSB 22.4 THE VARIOUS INTERIM COSTS ORDERS AND THEIR EFFECTS

[CPR Part 44]

The sessions dealing with this area of the syllabus on my BPTC course are	

You will recall from the chapter on costs that costs orders following any interim application will be subject to a summary assessment by the judge at the end of the interim hearing.

A short statement of costs must be served by the parties 24 hours before the hearing.

Activity

> Please refer back to the chapter on costs for what happens if
> this statement is not served. You may wish to copy it out again here.

Interim costs are payable within 14 days of them becoming due..

Possible interim cost orders are set out in the table at PD 44 in the section called "Court's discretion as to costs: rule 44.2" in the table in note 4.2

– Costs in any event

This means that in any event, no matter what the outcome of the final trial, the loser of the interim hearing pays the costs of the winner of the interim hearing.

Remember, however, the effect of QOCS where the claimant in a PI / fatal accidents case is the loser both at the interim hearing and at the final trial:

Because CPR rule 44.14 (2) says that QOCS can only be enforced 'after proceedings are concluded and costs have been assessed or agreed', then if the court does not award any damages or interest to C at the final trial because he is the loser there too, if C has not paid D's interim costs, D will be unable to enforce against C for payment of her interim costs.

– Costs in the case

This means that parties will 'wait-and-see' what the cost order is in the case at the end, then the loser in the final trial pays the other's costs of both the interim hearing and the final trial.

- **Costs reserved**

This means that the matter of costs will be deferred until the final trial. Should there be no costs order made at final trial, then the position will be costs in the case.

- **Claimant's/Defendant's costs in the case**

  - Claimant's costs in the case

1. C wins at interim hearing
2. C wins at final trial and is awarded costs
3. D pays C's costs of the interim hearing (and the rest of C's costs too).

Or

1. C wins at interim hearing
2. D wins at final trial and is awarded costs
3. D is not liable for C's interim costs, so C pays his own interim costs (and the rest of D's costs too)

  - Defendant's costs in the case

1. D wins at interim hearing
2. D wins at final trial and is awarded costs
3. C should pay D's costs of the interim hearing (and the rest of D's costs too) (subject to QOCS where relevant)

Or

1. D wins at interim hearing
2. C wins at final trial and is awarded costs
3. C is not liable for D's interim costs, so D pays her own interim costs (and the rest of C's costs too)

- **Costs thrown away**

The detail of this type of costs order was set out towards the end of chapter 12.

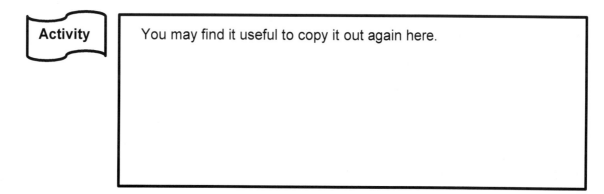

Activity — You may find it useful to copy it out again here.

– Costs of and caused by

The detail of this type of costs order was set out at the beginning chapter 15.

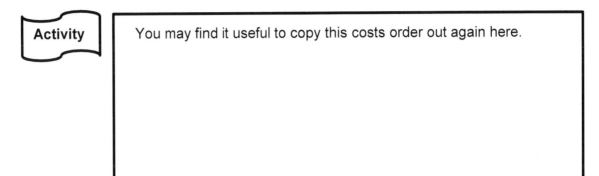

Activity | You may find it useful to copy this costs order out again here.

– Costs here and below

This is an order available to the Court of Appeal relating to costs both in that court and in the court from which the appeal was made.

– No order as to costs

Either where Counsel does not ask for an order as to costs or where the court chooses not to make one, each party bears their own costs of the interim application whatever costs order the court makes in relation to the final trial.

Chapter 21 MOCS

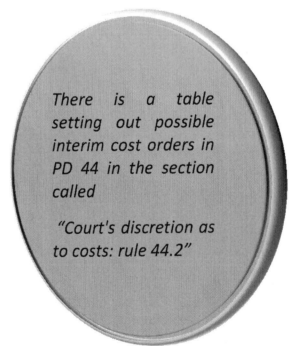

There is a table setting out possible interim cost orders in PD 44 in the section called

"Court's discretion as to costs: rule 44.2"

Chapter 22

p) Track Allocation, Court management of cases, Sanctions and relief from sanctions

CASE MANAGEMENT

[BSB 14; CPR Part 3, especially 3.8, 3.9, 3.12 – 3.18;

CPR Part 26 , especially 26.3 – 26.8,

CPR Part 27, especially 27.14, 27.8, PD 27; PD 28]

The sessions dealing with this area of the syllabus on my BPTC course are	

Having considered the "what-ifs" in the previous six chapters, we now pick up again from the end of chapter 15. In this current chapter we start from the point where the defence has been filed (and any "what –ifs" that have so far arisen have been dealt with).

The next stage of the process is the court giving notice to parties of which track it proposes to allocate the case to – the small claims track, the fast track or the multi-track, of which further detail later in this chapter.

BSB 14.1   The allocation of business between the small claims track, the fast track and the multi-track

1. Notice of the proposed track allocation

After all Ds have filed a defence / the time for filing the defence has expired, a court officer completes forms which are served on all parties giving notice of the proposed track allocation.

Contents of the notice

– A date by which the parties must file and serve the completed directions questionnaire
– A reminder that parties should consult one another and cooperate in the completion of the directions questionnaire
– A reminder that parties should try to agree the court management directions they will invite the court to make. In so doing the parties must have regard to those matters which are relevant to the procedural judge when (s)he makes the formal, final decision as to track allocation. These are set out in CPR 26.8 and include the amount of the claim, the remedy sought, the complexity of the facts/law, the number of parties. Note that at this stage consideration is not given to any amounts which are not in dispute, nor to interest, nor to costs, nor to whether there is a claim for contributory negligence. The court will approve the agreed court management directions that the parties invite the court to make if it finds them suitable.
– Where the proposed allocation is to the multi-track, the notice of proposed track allocation may specify the date for the filing of costs budgets. If it does not the latest date for doing so is 7 days before the first case management conference.

2. Directions questionnaires to be filed and served by the parties

– If proposed allocation is to the small claims track, at least 14 days after deemed service of notice of proposed allocation
– If proposed allocation is to the fast track or to the multi-track, at least 28 days after deemed service of notice of proposed allocation

- If any interim remedies are to be pursued, they must be notified to the court at this point
- If a party or parties wish to request a stay, a written request can be made to the court at this point. The stay will be for one month if all parties make the request. If the request does not come from all parties, the court, if it considers a stay appropriate, will direct that the whole or part of the proceedings are stayed for one month or such other period as it considers appropriate.

<u>Sanctions for not filing directions questionnaires</u>

- For **money only claims** the court serves a notice requiring it to be filed within an additional 7 days. Further non-compliance will lead to an automatic strike out.
- For **other types of claim** the court makes such order as it thinks appropriate. This could be the court
  - giving further directions; or
  - striking out the claim; or
  - striking out the defence and entering judgement; or
  - listing the matter for a case management conference.

3. <u>Formal allocation to track by a procedural judge by notice of allocation</u>

The procedural judge can allocate a claim to a lower track regardless of the wishes of the parties, e.g. if the claim is a straightforward one.

Likewise it may be that the CPR 26.8 relevant matters lead the procedural judge to allocate what initially looks like a case for the fast track, 'up' to the multi- track.

The directions given in the notice of allocation may include fixing a pre - trial review date.

Activity	Have a look at the costs chapter again and copy out here those claims likely to be allocated to
	<u>Small claims track</u>
	~
	~
	~
	<u>Fast track</u>
	~
	~
	~
	<u>Multi track</u>
	~
	~
	~

SMALL CLAIMS TRACK

- Where a claim would normally be allocated to the small claims track [**and** the claim is **not an RTA** claim, **PI** claim or **housing disrepair** claim], where all parties indicate on their directions questionnaire that they agree to mediation, the claim will be referred to the Mediation Service Small Claims Mediation Service operated by Her Majesty's Courts and Tribunals Service.

  If mediation brings about settlement the proceedings will automatically be stayed with permission to apply for
  - judgment for the unpaid balance of the outstanding sum of the settlement agreement; or
  - the claim to be restored for hearing of the full amount claimed,

  unless the parties have agreed that the claim is to be discontinued or dismissed.

  If the court has not been notified in writing that a settlement has been agreed, the claim will be allocated to a track no later than four weeks from the date on which the last directions questionnaire is filed.

- Small Claims are heard before a district judge in chambers. The atmosphere is informal. There are no strict rules of evidence. Evidence need not be on oath, the court may limit XX.

- Some CPRs do not apply. There are no interim remedies, no part 36 claims. Only the court, not the parties can require further information to be provided.

- **BSB 14.3 Typical directions in the small claims track** are referred to in the notice of allocation. Where the district judge specifies no other directions, standard directions are set out in Appendix B of PD27. They are that the parties must
  - Disclose documents on which they rely. (Disclosure is dealt with fully in the next chapter). Copies of these documents must be served (this will include the letter before claim and any reply, together with any expert reports) no later than 14 days before the hearing;
  - bring all <u>original</u> documents to the hearing
  - contact each other to try to settle
  - remember that they need to apply for the court's permission if they want to use an expert's report. On the small claims track, if it appears to the court that expert evidence is necessary, permission will be given for one expert jointly instructed by the parties. Appendix C of PD27 includes draft special directions for this.

FAST TRACK

- The trial is no longer than one day.
- In the notice of allocation the court either approves the case management directions agreed by the parties in the directions questionnaire or amends and then approves them.
- **BSB 14.3 Typical directions in fast track claims** are referred to in the notice of allocation. Directions on allocation are set out in PD28, note 3, with outline drafts in the Appendix. They deal with
  - Imposing a 30 week timetable to trial
  - Experts
    - Giving permission for the use of experts

- Directing that there be a single joint expert, unless there is a good reason not to do so, if both sides want an expert in the same field
- Using the expert's written report at trial; experts are directed to attend only if the court considers that it is in the interests of justice that they do so.
- Limiting oral expert evidence at trial to one expert each and to two fields (therefore 2 experts)
- Limiting the amount of fees recoverable from another party in respect of experts' fees
- Parties giving standard disclosure (this is explained in the next chapter)
- Giving the trial date.

The next stage of case management, where the court can give further directions will be when the pre-trial check lists are filed

MULTI-TRACK

- **BSB 14.3** Typical directions in multi-track claims
  - Again, parties must try to **agree** proposals for case management. There are specimen **directions** for multi-track claims on the Ministry of Justice website. Parties must try to agree directions **before any case management conference.**

    Case Management Conferences are conducted as a multi-track claim progresses towards trial. The first such slot is at this point. It can be vacated if the court approves what parties have agreed. This helps the overriding objective, saving time and money.

  - For PI multi-track cases, directions may be for standard disclosure, as explained in the next chapter, or directions will include much more court involvement than on the other tracks.

    For non-PI multi-track cases, there is a system called menu option disclosure as explained in the next chapter.

- **BSB 14.2** The procedure at case management conferences ("CMC")

If a legal representative attends a CMC, s/he must be familiar with the case, have sufficient ability and have the authority to agree outcomes on the client's behalf. If the legal representative is in adequate, not up to speed on all matters or without the authority to agree, there will be a wasted costs order against the party represented by that Counsel.

A CMC

- ensures the identification of the real **issues** between the parties
- identifies what **documents/evidence/experts** are necessary
- views the **cost budgets** (remember that the latest time for filing these is the date specified in the notice of allocation or if none, 7 days before first case management conference). **BSB 14.4** The impact of costs and the role of costs budgets in case management.

| Activity | Please refer back to the chapter on costs and note again here the section on the impact of costs and the role of costs budgets in case management. |

- records reasonable agreements in relation to what is at issue between the parties .
- lays down **directions**.
- can fix the date of a pre - trial review.

– Further case management conferences may be directed at any time up to the listing stage. These will
  - assess the progress of the case
  - assess whether initial directions have been complied with
  - review the steps taken by parties so far
  - review costs budgets
  - record any further agreements between the parties
  - lay down further directions

– [There is a section at the end of this chapter which deals with sanctions (e.g. for when a party fails to comply with directions) and then how a party can obtain relief from those sanctions]

– Continuing on with the workings of the multi-track - next, a **pre-trial checklist** is filed. If it appears that there are still issues to be addressed then there will be a pre-trial review.

– A **pre-trial review** is an additional hearing about 8 -10 weeks before the trial, conducted by the eventual trial judge at which further directions may be given.

It determines the timetable for the trial itself, for example setting time limits for opening speeches, XIC, XX, closing speeches, and for the consideration of the judgment.

It determines which expert evidence will be given solely on papers, or where oral expert evidence may be given.

If a legal representative attends a pre-trial review, the requirements are as for a case management conference set out above and failure by a legal adviser to meet those requirements may be subject to a wasted costs order.

- **The court sets the timetable.** It gives time estimate for the trial, directions re the organisation of the trial bundle, and fixes the period and place of trial. It is possible to transfer to a different trial centre

- **Trial.**

Where a party fails to comply with directions (for all tracks). BSB 16.2 The procedure for applying for sanctions, to strike out and for relief from sanctions, and the principles applied by the court

Although it is possible to apply for the court to strike out the case, **strike out is a sanction of last resort.**

Enforcement of a direction in the first instance is likely to be by way of an **"unless order"**

A must warn the other side of his intention to apply for an "unless order" before applying to the court for one under Part 23.

The court may order that unless the party complies with the direction within a certain timeframe, it will strike out that party's case and enter judgment for the other party. There is an example of such an order in 40BPD of the White Book in note 8 entitled "orders requiring an act to be done".

Where a rule, PD or court order requires a party to do something within a specified time and specifies the consequences of a failure to comply, CPR 3.8 (4) states that the time for doing the act in question may be extended by prior written agreement of the parties for up to a maximum of 28 days, without an application to the court provided that any such extension does not put at risk any hearing date. That is, unless the court orders otherwise.

In cases where the above paragraph does not apply, where a rule, PD or order states 'shall be struck out or dismissed' or 'will be struck out or dismissed' this means that the striking out or dismissal will be automatic and that no further order of the court is required.

Where the unless order relates to the whole of a statement of case being struck out, A can file a request for judgement with costs. The request must state that the right to enter judgement has arisen because the court's unless order has not been complied with. The claim will then be **struck out automatically**.

Where C is the party wishing to obtain judgment the claim will be automatically struck out when it is for any of the following
- a specified sum of money
- an amount of money to be decided by the court
- delivery of goods where the claim form gives D the alternative of paying their value (it will be judgement requiring D to deliver goods, or (if she does not do so) to pay the value of the goods as decided by the court (less any payments made); or
- any combination of these remedies
  D can apply not more than 14 days after receiving the judgement for relief from this sanction. The court will consider CPR 3.9 (Please see below).

QOCS

Remember that in a PI/fatal accident case where the strike out has been due to C's conduct there is no QOCS protection for C. Costs against C would therefore be enforceable to the full extent.

CPR 3.9

First, CPR 3.8 (1) sets out that where a party has failed to comply with a rule, PD or court order, sanctions have effect unless the defaulting party obtains relief from the sanction.

Rule 3.9 sets out the circumstances which the court will consider on an application to grant relief from a sanction. You have already met references to this in chapter 7, 12 and 14 of this book.

Relief from sanctions

When a court considers relief from sanctions, in addition to considering the overriding objective, [remember to include a full explanation of the overriding objective in your answer to any assessment question / pleadings in court] it considers the criteria in

- CPR 3.9 (1) ....all the circumstances of the case so as to enable it to deal justly with the application including the need
  - (a) for litigation to be conducted efficiently and at proportionate cost; and
  - (b) to enforce compliance with rules, PDs and orders.

  It is essential that (a) and (b) are considered in every case. The courts seem this year, with the introduction of this new form of CPR 3.9, to be considering the criteria in the following order.

- How serious has any non - compliance with rules, PDs or orders been?
  - Failure to pay court fees is always a serious breach (as litigation has not been conducted efficiently and at proportionate cost)
  - Breaches are likely to be considered all the more serious, the more that hearing dates and the litigation process have been disrupted (as litigation has not been conducted efficiently and at proportionate cost, yet even though there may not have been full compliance with the rules / PDs / orders, less serious non - compliance may not necessarily be a bar to obtaining relief from sanctions.

- How good was the reason for the non-compliance?
  - If the reason for non-compliance is considered a bad one it is likely to mean that litigation could not be conducted efficiently and at proportionate cost
  - Where circumstances were outside the control of the defaulting party, this is likely to be a good reason for non-compliance
  - Non-compliance, if the court considers there was a good reason for it, may not necessarily be a bar to obtaining relief from sanctions once all the circumstances of the case have been considered.

- All the circumstances of the case. These should include
  - how promptly the application was made and
  - any history of past breaches of other orders.

Defence served/time for doing so expired.

Court officer sends notice of proposed track allocation

Parties file and serve directions questionnaires

Formal track allocation by procedural judge

Case management on each of the tracks

Strike out, unless orders and relief from sanctions

Chapter 23

q) Disclosure and Inspection of Documents

EVIDENCE "I"

[BSB15, 27; CPR Part 31; CPR Part 82]

The sessions dealing with this area of the syllabus on my BPTC course are	

This is the first of four separate chapters on Evidence.

You will have learned in the previous chapter that the court gives directions on each of the three tracks, which involve directions about disclosure of documents.

BSB 15.1 The law, principles and procedure regulating disclosure and inspection of documents

First, some explanations.

A **document** is anything that is recorded. It therefore includes texts, e-mails, DVDs.

Disclose means setting out on a form for the other party that **documents exist or did exist** in relation to the claim.

Exist or did exist means that the document is or has been in the parties' physical control, or that the parties have the right to it, or have the right to inspect or take copies of it.

Menu option disclosure is the kind of disclosure used for **non-PI multi-track claims** unless the court orders otherwise.
- Stage I: disclosure report 14 days before the case management conference
- Stage II: discussion to agree the disclosure proposal
- Stage III: a case management conference disclosure order will be made

Standard Disclosure is set out in CPR 31.6. (Note that on the small claims track standard disclosure under CPR 31.6 is excluded and the court will direct that parties are only obliged to disclose documents on which they rely).

Standard disclosure is the usual direction on the **fast track** and for **PI claims in the multi-track**.

The court may direct otherwise for each of these cases, but where the direction is for standard disclosure this means, as set out in CPR 31.6, that parties must disclose

- Documents on which they rely and which
  - adversely affect their own case or another party's case or
  - support another party's case; plus
- Documents which a PD says must be disclosed

Parties have a duty to do a reasonable search; that is a search which is reasonable given

- the number of documents
- the nature and complexity of the proceedings
- how easy it will be to retrieve the documents; and

- the significance of document.

Once a party has seen the form completed by the other party disclosing the documents, it is likely the other party will wish to inspect some or all of the disclosed documents.

We will consider the form that the disclosure list takes before looking at how a party indicates their wish to inspect and at instances where they may not inspect some documents.

<u>How the disclosure list is set out</u>

After the headings, it begins with a **disclosure statement**
- confirming the extent to which documents have been searched for
- certifying that the disclosing party understands the duty to disclose
- certifying that that duty has been carried out during the search
- stating, where relevant, that one or more documents are not being disclosed, as to do so would be disproportionate; and stating why.

<u>Section 1 of the document giving disclosure</u>

Here a party discloses documents that exist, that they possess and that they do not object to the other party inspecting, as the disclosing party does not claim that the documents are privileged. (Privilege is explained in Section 2 below).

The party to whom they have been disclosed will give written notice of their wish to inspect these documents. They must be permitted to inspect them within 7 days of the notice of the wish to inspect. Inspection will either be of the originals at the offices of either party, or copies will be sent, each party undertaking to cover reasonable copying charges.

Disclosed documents may only be used for the purposes of the proceedings in which they are disclosed unless **(BSB15.3** <u>Collateral use of disclosed documents</u>)
- they are read in open court (are in the public domain); or
- the disclosing party agrees to their collateral use; or
- the court gives permission for their collateral use.

BSB 27.6   <u>Use of secondary facts,</u>

If one party inadvertently provides a privileged document for inspection to the other side, the disclosing party can try for an injunction to stop the other side using it, if there is no equitable reason for a court not to grant one e.g. delay/misconduct on the disclosing party's part. Such an injunction may be granted where
- the other party got the document by fraud or
- there was an obvious mistake in revealing the document to them.

The party who inspected the document can only use it with the court's permission.

<u>Section 2 of the document giving disclosure</u>

Here a party discloses documents that exist, that they possess but that they **do object** to the other party inspecting, as the disclosing party claims that the documents are privileged.

When a party claims that a document is privileged, that party is asserting a right or duty to withhold them from inspection.

BSB 27.7 The principles relating to legal professional privilege, privilege against self-incrimination, without prejudice communications and public interest immunity in civil cases, and exceptions to these rules

There are four types of privilege; legal professional privilege, without prejudice communications, public interest immunity and the privilege against self-incrimination.

– Legal Professional Privilege. There are two types.

- **legal advice privilege,** relating to **any legal advice between** lawyer/client
- **litigation privilege,** covering documents between lawyer/client/third-party (witness) where the document was
  - for use in pending contemplated or existing litigation
  - where the **dominant purpose** at the time the document was **created** is
  - for use in **these proceedings**.

BSB 27.8 Waiver of privilege The party to whom Legal Professional Privilege relates can waive the privilege if they wish.

– Without prejudice communications. Parties can claim privilege for documents containing any genuine attempt at settlement. It is not necessary to state the words "without prejudice" for a document to be such a communication. Similarly, merely stating that a document is "without prejudice" does not make it such a document if it is not a genuine attempt to settle!

BSB 27.8 Waiver of privilege Both parties have the privilege, so both consents to waiver are needed if the privilege is to be waived.

– Public Interest Immunity. This is where it is claimed that the public interest is best furthered by not disclosing a class of documents, or a particular document.

Where a party would be required to disclose sensitive material harmful to national security if disclosed, (or would be so required if not claiming Public Interest Immunity), a court may make a declaration that the that the proceedings are proceedings in which a "closed material application" may be made to the court, applying for permission not to disclose material otherwise than to
- the court,
- any person appointed as a special advocate, and
- the Secretary of State, where the Secretary of State is not the applicant but is a party to the proceedings.

The Ministry of Defence can certify that a court should not allow inspection of the documents if the certificate shows an actual risk to national security. The court may in its discretion review the claim to the immunity if satisfied that there is a strong case for the documents to be disclosed and that public interest is best furthered by disclosure, balancing whether the party wanting disclosure persuades the court that the public interest is best served by disclosure so that justice can be done, with whether it is more in the public interest that the documents are not disclosed.

BSB 27.8 Waiver of privilege The party to whom Public Interest Immunity relates can waive the privilege if they wish.

– Privilege against self-incrimination A party may refrain from incriminating him or herself OR their spouse, although the privilege is not available for IP or passing off cases, theft, fraud, or care of children cases.

The party to whom the privilege belongs may waive it if they wish.

<u>Section 3 of the document giving disclosure</u>

Here a party discloses documents that did exist - they no longer have them; for example they have already been sent the other side or they have been lost or destroyed.

After this first disclosure, remember that the **duty to disclose is ongoing** so parties may need to do additional lists later.

BSB 15.2   The principles and procedure relating to specific disclosure

Where a party is aware that the other party has a document that does not appear on the disclosure list, that party can apply for an order for specific disclosure of that specific document. The Part 23 application may be for
- documents or classes of documents to be disclosed
- a search to be carried out (the required extent of the search will be stated in the order)
- any documents located as a result of the search to be disclosed

Similarly an order for specific inspection allowing a party to inspect one of the above documents can be made.

In exercising its discretion the court considers
- all the circumstances of the case
- the overriding objective
- the relevance of the documents sought, by looking at the statements of case
- whether the documents are or have been in the parties' control, by looking at the statements of case

BSB 15.5   Disclosure against non parties

Proceedings must have started; so once they have, a party can apply to the court for an order that a witness produce documents in advance of the trial. Such an order will only be made if
- the documents are likely to support A's case / adversely affect one or other of the parties
- AND it is necessary to dispose of the case fairly or save costs.

The witness can be brought to the trial with the original document by means of a witness summons. These are dealt with in the next chapter.

CPR 36.1 standard disclosure for fast track and PI multi-track claims unless the court directs otherwise.

Menu option disclosure for non-PI multi-track unless the court directs otherwise

Right to inspect documents unless privileged.

Chapter 24

q) Witness statements, Witness Summary, Depositions, Hearsay

EVIDENCE "II"

[BSB 27, BSB 21; CPR Parts 32, 33, 34]

The sessions dealing with this area of the syllabus on my BPTC course are	

We have already seen that where facts need to be proved by witness evidence at hearings **other than trials**, such as Part 23 interim applications, the evidence is provided **in writing** with the application, (unless the CPR or a court order says otherwise).

Where facts need to be proved by witness evidence at **trials**, the evidence is provided by the witness ("W") **orally in public** (unless a court orders otherwise).

Courts may allow evidence at trials to be given by video link or other means.

Any evidence that W would be allowed to give orally in court will most commonly be set out in the form of a witness statement. The court will have included in its directions how witness statements are to be dealt with in the case. Most commonly, a witness will be questioned on the basis of their witness statement. In the civil courts, the witness statement stands as XIC unless the court orders otherwise. So if nothing has changed since the witness statement was served, that witness will not be questioned by their own Counsel at the beginning of the case.

More detail about witness statements now follows.

BSB 27.4   The practice and procedure relating to the preparation and exchange of witnesses statements

- A **witness statement** is a signed statement of witness evidence that W would be allowed to give orally in court. It must contain a **statement of truth** and be **signed by W**. Therefore a lot of weight is given to witness statements.

- When the court gives directions it may set out
  - whether or not witness statements are to be filed. They are filed in the court where the CF was issued / where proceedings are now proceeding if that is different
  - the witnesses who may be called or whose evidence may be read
  - the issues to which factual evidence may be directed
  - the length or format of witness statements
  - the order in which witness statements are to be served
  - by when witness statements are to be served if parties intend to rely on them at trial
  - [If not served in time, court permission is needed to call W to give oral evidence]

– Format of witness statements

Activity

You should refer to case studies given to you by your Provider for examples of well- drafted witness statements.

Please refer to 32PD.17-20 and make notes here on the format of witness statements.

– At trial, if new matters have arisen since the witness statement was served on the other parties, Counsel should ask the court's **permission to amplify** the witness statement. The court is likely to grant this if it considers there is a good reason to do so. Counsel will then conduct XIC so that W can give evidence in relation to these matters and get them before the court.

- Where the court has directed a party to serve a witness statement for use at trial, but that party has been unable to obtain one from the relevant witness, the party may **apply** without notice **for permission** to serve a **witness summary** instead.
  - if the party knows what the relevant witness would say in evidence, the party then states that evidence in the witness summary
  - if the party does not know what the relevant witness would say in evidence, the party states the matters about which they propose to question the witness
  - it follows that there is no statement of truth in a witness summary. It thus carries less weight than a witness statement.

- Say, for example that a key witness is ill or unable to travel, or abroad, the solution is a **deposition**. (If W is outside the jurisdiction a letter of request must be sent to the judicial authorities of the country they are in).

  - A applies for an order that the witness be examined before the hearing. (See further the chapter called "Evidence at trial" later in this book). W is called the deposer and will be on oath before a judge/court examiner/court appointed person. The deposer gets expenses for making the deposition.
  - The deposition is what the witness would have said in evidence in trial. A full copy of the deposition is sent to A and to the court.
  - If a witness served with a deposition order either fails to attend or refuses to attend or answer any questions, the examiner will certify this and the certificate will be filed by A.
  - Notice of the deposition must be served on every other party at least 21 days before the hearing. The deposition is then treated as a witness statement.

BSB 27.3   The law and practice relating to the admission of hearsay evidence in civil trials

Hearsay evidence is **admissible**: Civil Evidence Act 1995.

Hearsay is "a statement tendered as evidence of the matters stated made otherwise than by a person whilst giving oral evidence proceedings".

If a witness is not giving oral evidence at court, their witness statement and exhibits, (or other documents such as letters, emails, texts, maps, photos which are not part of exhibits to witness statements), could alternatively be put in as hearsay evidence.

If the evidence includes business records, they must be certified by an officer of the business, to be admissible.

If the party who served a witness statement does not use it either orally or as hearsay evidence, any other party can put it in as hearsay evidence.

- Procedure

  - **Serve** the witness statement and exhibits (or just the other documents if they are not exhibited to a witness statement) on the other parties within the timeframe directed by the court **with notice** that the witness statement (or documents) will be put in as **hearsay** evidence. The notice should state why W is not being called to give oral evidence.

  - If the notice is not served, hearsay evidence is still admissible, although it may affect the weight attached to it and any costs order.

  - Supply copy documents to any party who requests them.

- Not more than 14 days after service of the hearsay notice, the other side can nevertheless apply to court for permission to XX that witness

- In the same timeframe another party can give **notice** to the party proposing to give the hearsay statement in evidence of their **intention** to call evidence **to attack the credibility** of the person whose evidence is to be presented as hearsay.

– Weight given to hearsay evidence

- The court has regard to any circumstances from which an **inference** can be reasonably drawn **as to the reliability** or otherwise **of the evidence**. Such circumstances are
  o The ease with which the person who made the statement could have been brought to court. It should be easy to produce a person living round the corner, harder or impossible if the person is abroad or dead. Less weight will be given to the hearsay evidence of a person living round the corner;
  o How close in time the hearsay evidence was created to the actual event being evidenced. More weight is given to a note of a car registration number taken at the scene of the accident than to a note made of it from memory several hours later;
  o The greater the number of hearsay evidences in a case, the less weight they will lend to the case;
  o Does any person involved have a motive to conceal/misrepresent
  o Was the original statement an edited account
  o do circumstances suggest an attempt to prevent the proper evaluation of the weight of the hearsay evidence.
  o Whether due notice of the hearsay was given

BSB 27.5   The principles underlying the general exclusionary rule in relation to evidence of opinion and the main exceptions to that rule

Evidence which is the **personal opinion** of the witness is **not admissible.** That is **unless**
– W is an expert witness opining on something within their expertise.
– The personal opinion of a non-expert is the only way that the relevant fact they personally perceived can be expressed. e.g. W giving his/her opinion in an RTA related claim that a vehicle was travelling far too fast.

Chapter 24 MOCS

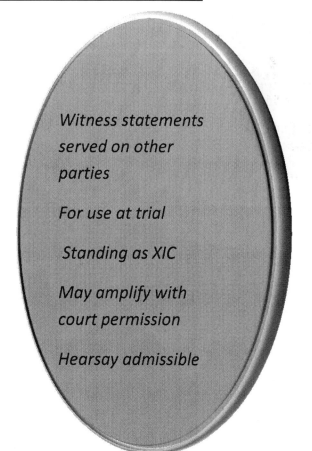

Witness statements served on other parties

For use at trial

Standing as XIC

May amplify with court permission

Hearsay admissible

Chapter 25

g) Expert Evidence

EVIDENCE "III"

[BSB 27; CPR Part 35]

The sessions dealing with this area of the syllabus on my BPTC course are	

BSB 27.6   The definition of an expert

An expert
- does not need to be formally qualified. They may be an expert due to skills acquired through experience
- opines on their area of expertise, restricted to what is reasonably required to resolve the proceedings
- has a primary duty to the court

BSB 27.6   The requirements for permission to use expert evidence and to call experts

- Applications for court permission to call an expert or put in an expert's report, need to identify
  - the field in which expert evidence is required (reasonably required, that is, to enable proceedings to be finalised, being relevant to a matter in dispute between the parties) and
  - where practicable the name of the expert (with details of qualifications/experience);
  - the amount of costs with a **costs estimate**

- Permission on the small claims track is for one expert on one issue

- Permission on the other tracks
  - if both sides want an expert in the same field, unless there is a good reason not to, the court can direct that there is a single joint expert,. Oral expert evidence at trial is limited to one expert each and two fields (therefore 2 experts)
  - it is often the written report that is that used at trial; experts are directed to attend only if the court considers it would be in the interests of justice if they did.

- The court may limit the amount of fees recoverable from another party in relation to an expert's fees

BSB 27.6   The special rules relating to the opinion of experts,

- The court may direct that there be concurrent expert evidence (hot-tubbing) and that parties agree an agenda for this, usually structured according to the areas of disagreement.

- Procedure
  - Experts from similar disciplines each take the oath/affirm
  - They give evidence concurrently on each agenda item as follows (unless the court orders otherwise)

- o The judge asks each in turn their view, each in turn expresses that view and the judge may ask questions/ask another expert to comment/ask another expert to question the expert whom the judge initially asked
- o This is repeated for every expert
- o Next, parties' representatives can ask questions of the experts
- o Then the judge may summarise the experts' different positions and ask them to confirm or correct the summary

- Where a court did not direct a single joint expert or all parties cannot agree on a single one, the court may direct that
  - expert reports are exchanged. (Failure to exchange means that unless the court gives permission, the report may not be used at trial / the expert may not be called to give evidence at trial).
  - the experts meet to identify the issues and agree an opinion were possible
  - the experts prepare a report setting out where they agree or disagree and why.

BSB 27.6   The form of experts' reports

They need to
- be addressed to the court
- set out the expert's qualifications or experience
- give details of literature relied on in making the report
- set out the substance of the facts and instructions material to the opinions in the report
- show which facts are in the expert's own knowledge
- identify, giving their qualifications, anyone who may have for example carried out tests the results of which are contained in the report, and whether the expert supervised the tests
- set out the range of the expert's opinion
- draw attention to anything the expert wishes to qualify in the report
- summarise the conclusions reached
- confirm that the expert understands his/her duties to the court
- confirm that the expert has complied with that duty
- contain a **statement of truth**

| Activity | Copy out here 35PD.3 note 3.3, the prescribed form of the **statement of truth** for expert reports. |

"I confirm that I have made clear which facts + matters referred to in this report are within my own knowledge and which are not, those that are within my own knowledge I confirm to be true. The opinions I have expressed represent my true and complete professional opinions on the matters to which they refer."

Within 28 days of service of the report written questions may be put to the expert once to clarify the report. The responses become part of the report. (Failure to reply to the clarification questions means that the party instructing the expert may not rely on the expert evidence/may not recover from another party the fees and expenses of that expert).

BSB 27.6   Disclosure of reports and literature

- Reports

  Where our own expert provides a report unfavourable to our client, this must be disclosed, although we can withhold inspection of it as it is privileged, being in contemplation of litigation.

  Where a subsequent new expert report is commissioned, the court usually orders the initial unfavourable report to be disclosed as a condition for giving permission to rely on a new expert's report

- Literature e.g. coaching an expert as to what you want them to include

  The court only orders disclosure if it is satisfied that there are reasonable grounds for needing clarification of what the instructions to the expert actually were. The court will allow XX on this if it appears to be in the interests of justice to do so.

BSB 27.6   Ultimate issues

The ultimate issues rule is that there are some issues on which only the court can have the ultimate adjudication.

For instance this is the case where the court is highly sceptical of certain expert evidence and the expert's opinions go to issues on which only the court can adjudicate.

Thus the opinion of an expert may not always be the ultimate resolution on a matter.

Chapter 25 MOCS

Expert's duty is to the court

Need Court permission

Form of report

Expert meetings

Hot- tubbing

Apply rules on privilege from inspection for unfavourable reports by our own expert

Chapter 26

g) Evidence at trial

EVIDENCE "IV"

[BSB 27]

The sessions dealing with this area of the syllabus on my BPTC course are	

BSB 27.1   Burden and standard of proof [but not presumptions or judicial notice]

Standard of Proof

The standard of proof in civil cases is "**on the balance of probabilities**". That means that if the judge can say "I think it is more probable than not" then the standard is met and the case proven; but if the probabilities are equal, the standard is not met.

Burden of Proof

Matters must be proved by the person who asserts those matters: "**He who asserts must prove**". So

- C in the main claim
- D when alleging C's contributory negligence
- D when alleging C's failure to mitigate
- D when counterclaiming against C
- D when the claim is under s.2 (1) Misrepresentation Act 1967, must show that "D had reasonable grounds to believe and did believe up to the time of the contract that the facts represented were true".

BSB 27.2   Competence and compellability of witnesses

Competence

A witness is competent if they may be called to give evidence. A witness may be called to give evidence if they are suitable or able. So

- Children
  - **Sworn** evidence if the child has sufficient appreciation of/understands the solemnity of the occasion AND understands the added responsibility to tell the truth over and above the ordinary social duty to do so. This is the **Hayes test.**
  - **Unsworn** evidence otherwise, if the child understands the duty to speak the truth and has sufficient understanding to justify their evidence being heard

- Persons of unsound mind or defective intellect
  - **Sworn** evidence **only** so they must pass the Hayes test. The judge/jury will attach such weight to the evidence as they see fit.

Compellability

A competent witness is a compellable one and so may be brought to court in the usual ways, set out in chapter 27 of this book.

BSB27.9 Evidence rules governing examination in chief and cross-examination, comprising: leading and non-leading questions; cross-examination as to credit, the rule of finality, and exceptions to that rule, hostile and unfavourable witnesses; and use of previous consistent and inconsistent evidence.

Again, reference to your advocacy sessions is advised.

XIC of your own witness

Counsel for C asks C to identify his witness statement, directing him to the statement of truth and asking him to confirm that the signature is his. You will recall from chapter 24 that unless the court orders otherwise, witness statements stand as XIC;

Also from chapter 24 you will recall that amplification is possible with court permission, thus allowing Counsel to ask further oral questions.

Counsel uses non-leading questions [e.g. "who, what, when, where, why?" questions] (although Counsel may ask leading questions to elicit yes/no answers where facts are not disputed or the court has given permission since the witness is a hostile one or if Counsel for the other side does not object). Less weight is given to responses where leading questions are asked.

Hostile and unfavourable witnesses

Hostile witness

- A W is hostile when it is your own witness who fails to say what is expected during questioning in court / shows no desire to tell the truth to the court.

- Counsel for the party calling the witness
  - needs court permission to treat them as hostile
  - can ask the witness to refresh his memory from the witness statement
  - may then XX the witness. Counsel will call other evidence to show that W said something different previously.

- **Use of previous inconsistent evidence** Counsel will ask W whether or not he has previously made this different statement, inconsistent to the statement he has just made in court.

If W sticks to the previous inconsistent statement then this is part of his evidence. The previous inconsistent statement is admissible as evidence of the truth of its contents.

If W does not admit to making the earlier inconsistent statement, it is up to the court to accept either version.

The previous inconsistent statement may not be used so as to discredit the witness generally.

Unfavourable witness

A W is unfavourable when it is your own witness who fails to come up to proof in court or gives evidence that is unfavourable. Counsel may call other witnesses to give evidence of those matters. When questioning your own unfavourable witness, it may not be so as to discredit this W generally.

Use of previous consistent evidence

If there are any allegations by the other side that evidence has recently been fabricated, a previous statement made by a witness that you are calling which is entirely consistent with their evidence at trial can be used as evidence of the matters stated within it and as evidence of consistency.

Such statements are hearsay and prima facie admissible. [See chapter 24].

BSB 27.10   Character evidence

If the other side has attacked the credibility of your witness, (see XX as to credit below), Counsel can bring evidence of the good character of your witness to rebut that.

Good character evidence is also admissible if this is the fact in issue or if it is relevant to the fact in issue.

When questioning your own witness, Counsel may not bring evidence of W's bad character.

XX of the other side's witness

Lead, lead in XX !

Questions posed on XX are subject to the **discretion of the judge** who will **prevent any irrelevant, improper, disproportionate or oppressive** questions.

XX as to credit

- Counsel will be trying to show that the character of the **opponent's witness** is such that she **ought not to be believed**. This may be due to errors, exaggeration, inconsistencies, mistakes or omissions in her evidence; or discreditable conduct, unspent convictions, or spent convictions where justice cannot be done without admitting them as evidence. [Spent convictions are generally not admissible].

- **CEA 1968, s. 11 = convictions as evidence in civil proceedings. Unspent** convictions are **admissible** in evidence for the purpose of proving that a person committed that offence. A convicted person is taken to have committed that offence unless the contrary is proved.

- Counsel may ask any question, the answers to which would seriously affect the opinion of the court on the witness's credibility if they were true.

The rule of finality and the exceptions to it

Collateral issues are those that are directly relevant to the facts at issue, so, for instance, credit (belief) of the evidence of the other side's witness.

Answers to questions concerning a **collateral issue are final**. Counsel who is XXing cannot call further evidence to prove the contrary, although the court is not obliged to accept the answer given by the witness as true.

Where, however, W answers in the negative, questions on

- whether she has previous unspent convictions,
- is biased,
- has a physical or mental disability that affects reliability, or

– whether she has been untruthful in the past

Counsel can bring evidence to rebut the negative answer.

Use of previous inconsistent evidence

– No permission is needed for this.
– Please refer to notes on this point in the section on hostile witnesses above. The same is the case for previous inconsistent statements when XXing the other side's witness; in addition to being evidence of the truth of the contents of the previous inconsistent statement, **it also goes to impugn the credibility of the witness**.

BSB 27.10   Character evidence

Evidence of the bad character of a W or of the bad character of a non-party is admissible if this is the fact in issue or if it is relevant to the fact in issue and potentially probative of that fact.

If the other side has attacked the credibility of your witness, (see XX as to credit above), Counsel can bring evidence of the good character of this witness to rebut that.

Chapter 26 MOCS

NB: further evidence may be adduced after the end of the trial and before judgement is given if the judge considers it is in the interests of justice to do so !!

Children and those with mental incapacity give sworn evidence if they pass the Hayes test;

Children may also give unsworn evidence

Evidence and witnesses at trial

Chapter 27

r) TRIAL

[BSB 21; CPR Parts 39 and 40]

The sessions dealing with this area of the syllabus on my BPTC course are	

BSB 21.1   The use of witness summonses

A court will serve a witness summons to compel W to attend at court or to produce a document in their possession at court. It is also possible for the summons to be served by personal service.

A witness summons is binding if served at least 7 days before the document or attendance at trial is required.

It may be served later than this with court permission.

W has a right to reasonable expenses for travel to and from court and for loss of time.

Failure to attend court following a witness summons is contempt of court, punishable by a fine/prison.

BSB 21.2   Skeleton arguments

You will learn how to skeleton arguments on the BPTC. They are compulsory for High Court trials. Directions in the County Court may also require them.

Skeleton arguments are a concise summary of submissions to be made on the issues raised in the claim; they should not be a paper argument on the whole case. They set out the authorities which will be relied upon. A list of the authorities should be provided to the other side as far in advance of the hearing is possible.

BSB 21.3   The procedure on the trial of civil cases in all tracks, including trial timetables, the order of speeches, calling and examining witnesses

Fast track Timetable

In consultation with the parties, as soon as practicable after

– the date specified for filing the pre-trial checklist

the court will
- fix the date for the trial;
- give directions it considers appropriate, including the trial timetable; and
- specify any further steps that need to be taken before trial.

The court will give at least 3 weeks' notice of the trial date, although shorter notice can be given in exceptional circumstances.

Multi-track timetable

In consultation with the parties, as soon as practicable after

- each party has filed the completed pre-trial checklist; or
- the court has held a listing hearing; or
- the court has held the pre-trial review following receipt of the parties' pre-trial check lists

the court will
- set the timetable to trial unless it considers it inappropriate to do so;
- set the trial date / the week for trial to begin; and
- notify parties of the trial timetable and the date or period for it.

Trial bundle

Unless the court orders otherwise, **C** files it not more than 7 and not less than 3 clear days before the start of the trial.

39APD.3 provides a list of what they should contain. Otherwise a court order will set this out.

Procedure

Trial hearings are in public unless they involve e.g. national security, or it is necessary to protect the interests of a child or a protected party. In such cases they may be in private.

Order of speeches

C opening speech

C's case

XIC of C. (Remember that the witness statement stands as XIC. Remember that there may be XIC on new matters if C's counsel obtains court permission to amplify.

XX of C. This may include **calling and examining witnesses.** Please refer to the earlier chapters called "EVIDENCE "II"" and "EVIDENCE IV")

Re-examination

D may submit no case to answer

D's case

XIC of D. (Remember that the witness statement stands as XIC. Remember that there may be XIC on new matters if C's counsel obtains court permission to amplify. This amplification may include **calling and examining witnesses.** Please refer to the earlier chapters called "EVIDENCE "II"" and "EVIDENCE IV")

XX of D. This may include **calling and examining witnesses.** Please refer to the earlier chapters called "EVIDENCE "II"" and "EVIDENCE IV")

Re-examination

D closing speech

C closing speech

Judgement (either now or deferred/reserved until later)

Submissions on costs

Order as to costs

Application for permission to appeal can be made orally at this point. (See the later chapter on appeals).

BSB 21.4   Submissions on orders for costs

Remember that if an order makes no mention of costs then each party will bear their own costs. So Counsel must include submissions as to costs to persuade the court to exercise its discretion in the client's favour where appropriate.

Thus the Particulars of Claim ("POC") will include

- the authority for claiming the interest (either s.69 County Courts Act 1984 or s.35A Senior Courts Act 1981 if you are in the High Court)
- the period covered by the interest (the date when a successful C should have been paid until the date he is paid; therefore from the date of loss to the date of judgment).

   Where the claim is for a specific sum of money, the Particulars of Claim will show the daily rate of interest at $1/365^{th}$ (even in a leap year) and will provide that interest continues to accrue at this daily rate until it is paid in full.

- the rate of interest (usually pitched at the 8% taken from the Judgments Act 1838 – see below).

Worked example of interest on a debt claim

Suppose that C is claiming for a debt of £5,600 and that 140 days have passed since the debt became due and the POC is being drafted.

C will claim £5,600 + interest at 8% per annum.

1% per annum would be £5600/100 = £56; so 8% per annum = £56 x 8 = £448

If the debt were repaid exactly a year later, interest on it would be £448; so we need to calculate what that equates to per day. £448/365 = £1.227p per day.

The daily rate is £1.227.

At the date of drafting the POC, C is owed £1.227p x 140 days = £171.78 in interest.

So the POC will claim "interest pursuant to section 69 of the County Courts Act 1984 on the sum of £5,600.00 from 10th June [year] at the rate of 8% per annum, amounting to £171.78 at 29th October [year] and continuing at the daily rate of £1.23 until judgment or sooner payment."

BSB 8.4   The law and practice in respect of interest on judgment debts pursuant to contract or statute (Judgments Act 1838; County Court (Interest on Judgment Debts) Order 1991

Unpaid judgment debts will also be subject to interest as set out in the 1838 Act and 1991 Order. Interest runs from the date that judgement is given unless a PD says differently or the court orders otherwise.

The Act provides for a rate of 8% per annum from date of judgment. Where the claim is for a specific amount the daily rate to judgment is likely to be used. If the claim is not for a specific amount, the Particulars of Claim will ask for such interest as the court thinks fit.

BSB 8.4   Late Payment of Commercial Debts (Interest) Act 1998).

Statutory Interest

For contracts which are for the supply of goods or services where the purchaser and the supplier are each acting in the course of a business, (though not for consumer credit agreements or contracts relating to mortgages) there is an implied term that on the **'qualifying' i.e. commercial debt**, the contract carries simple interest, referred to as **statutory interest**, if interest is otherwise not available.

Statutory interest of 8% above the Bank of England Base Rate starts to run on the day after the day on which the debt is to be created by the contract; or

- where the debt relates to an obligation to make an advance payment, the relevant day is the day on which the debt is treated by the Act as having been created.
- in any other case, the relevant day is the last day of the period of **30 days** beginning with whichever is the later of
  - the day on which the obligation of the supplier to which the debt relates is **performed**; or
  - the day on which the purchaser has **notice of the amount** of the debt or (where that amount is unascertained) the sum which the supplier claims is the amount of the debt.

Remission of statutory interest.

Where, by reason of any **conduct,** act or omission of the supplier, the interests of justice require that statutory interest should be **remitted in whole or part** in respect of a period for which it would otherwise run in relation to a qualifying debt then the supplier may receive no statutory interest or statutory interest at a reduced rate for a period.

Fixed sum

Once statutory interest begins to run in relation to a qualifying debt, the supplier shall be entitled to **a fixed sum**, relative to the amount of the debt (**in addition to the statutory interest** on the debt).

Submissions on orders for permission to appeal

Following a ruling in a lower court, application may be made orally at the end of that hearing where permission to appeal is required. The test to be satisfied is RPOS or SOCR [Please see the later chapter on appeals].

Please refer further to your advocacy course on these matters.

Chapter 27 NO MOCS !

Chapter 28

s) JUDGMENTS AND ORDERS

[BSB 23, BSB 9; CPR Part 40]

The sessions dealing with this area of the syllabus on my BPTC course are	

BSB 23.1 **Who, generally, is responsible for drawing up a judgment / order, together with exceptions to the general rule**

– Judgements or orders made by a court of its own initiative are drawn up by the court

– Unless the court orders otherwise
  • those made in QBD are drawn up by the parties
  • those made in the Administrative Court are drawn up by the court

– Unless the court or a PD orders otherwise, every other judgement or order will be drawn up by the court, although the court may order a party to draw it up. That party must file the judgment / order at court within 7 days of the date when it was ordered to draw it up.

BSB 23.2 **The consequences where a party fails to draw up and file a judgment / order within the time permitted**

Any other party may draw it up and file it. Either the court will check it or it will ask the parties to file an agreed statement of the terms of the judgment / order before it is drawn up and sealed.

BSB 9.3 **The impact of Social Security payments on the assessment of damage**

– Please refer back to the end of the chapter called "Remedies, contract and tort".

– The preamble to the judgement / order will state the amount by which it is being reduced to take account of recoverable benefits received by C.

BSB 23.6 **The form of orders requiring an act to be done**

– Please remind yourself of the reference to 40BPD in chapter 22 where we referred to 40BPD of the White Book, note 8, "orders requiring an act to be done" in relation to unless orders.

– Consent judgements and orders. The order must be
  • drawn up in the terms agreed
  • expressed as being "By Consent"
  • signed by the legal representative for each of the parties to whom the order relates
  • signed by the party if he has applied for the judgment/order as a litigant in person

– Where all parties agree the terms the court officer may enter and seal an agreed judgement if
  • the judgment / order is listed in CPR 40.6(3);
  • none of the parties is a litigant in person; and
  • the approval of the court is not required

- Where the preceding two points do not apply, any party may apply for a judgment / order in the terms agreed.

- Judgements or orders take effect from the day when they are given or made or such later date as the court may specify.

BSB 23.3   The time for payment of a money judgment

Payment, including costs should be made within 14 days of the judgement or order unless

- it specifies a different date;
- a CPR rule specifies a different date; or
- the court has stayed the claim.

BSB 23.4   Penal notices in interim injunction orders

Please see the earlier chapter on interim injunctions.

BSB 23.5   Tomlin orders

It is likely that you met these on your ADR/ReDOC course. They are used for confidential or complex matters.

Details of the agreement are not shown on the face of the order, only in the private schedule. Costs are shown on the face of the order. When a Tomlin order is made, proceedings are stayed with "liberty to apply". This simply means that the party has liberty to apply to court to get the stay lifted so that the terms in the schedule can be carried into effect. When enforcing a Tomlin order, this is the first stage. The second stage of the enforcement of the order is by using one of the usual methods of enforcement. These are set out in the next chapter on enforcement of judgments.

Chapter 28 MOCS

Rules as to who draws up the judgement or order

Consent orders

Tomlin orders

Chapter 29

t) ENFORCEMENT OF JUDGMENTS

[BSB24; CPR Parts 72, 83 AND 84]

The sessions dealing with this area of the syllabus on my BPTC course are	

BSB 24.1   **The different methods of enforcing money and other judgments (in outline); and**

BSB 24.2   **Which method or combination of methods is appropriate to the particular circumstances of the judgment debtor in question.**

[NB This topic will be assessed at the level of junior counsel advising a client on enforcement immediately after a fast track trial.]

ENFORCEMENT OF MONEY ORDERS

When the losing party does not comply with the judgement, there are ways to enforce it through the courts. A debtor can ask the court for a stay of execution to give her time to pay.

Where a judgment creditor does not know what assets the judgment debtor owns, he may apply to the County Court hearing centre for the judgment debtor's home / business address for a court order to obtain information from the debtor.

Methods of enforcement

These are
– Taking control of goods
– Charging order
– Third Party Debt order
– Attachment of earnings

County Court = taking control of goods = <£5k charging order = third party debt order = attachment of earnings	High Court = taking control of goods = >£5k charging order = third party debt order
>£600 can transfer to High	
>£5k control of goods must transfer to High must →	
>£350k debt; charging order being enforced by sale must →	
← must	<£600 control of goods
← must	<£5k by charging order for debt
← must	Attachment of earnings order
Enforcement by enforcement agents	**Enforcement by enforcement officers**

A judgement creditor can choose any one or all of the methods either concurrently or consecutively. Factors affecting the choice of method or methods of execution will depend what assets the judgement debtor has and also how quickly the judgement creditor wishes or needs to get hold of the money.

<u>Taking control of goods</u>

This is when the enforcement agent or enforcement officer removes / secures goods to the value of the debt owed in order to sell them; or enters into a controlled goods agreement with the judgment debtor. Any removal, securing or agreement does not include domestic appliances or 'tools of the trade' of which they may not take control.
They can use only reasonably necessary force at the home/place of business of the judgment debtor and entry must be via a door or normal place of entry.

Do take special note of the names of the methods of enforcement in the box above:
Warrant of control in **County** Court; or
Writ of control in **High** Court.
Both are valid for 12 months.

The judgment creditor makes a request to court with draft warrant or writ of control and pays the fee.

At least 7 clear days' notice in prescribed form is given by the enforcement agent/officer to the debtor at her home or business address.

If this prompts payment, the property is returned. If this does not prompt the judgment debtor to pay, she is given 7 clear days' notice of the sale by auction of the controlled goods, following valuation.

<u>Charging Order</u>

This is an order obtained from the court to put a charge on an asset. This acts as security for the money judgment. You may remember charges and mortgages on the charges register of registered properties from your pre – BPTC studies. This charge would be put on there and so may not be a first charge if there is a pre-existing mortgage or charge on the property. A judgement creditor may be running the risk of there being insufficient funds to pay his second or later charge once the first or previous charges on the property have been settled if he chooses this method of enforcement against real property.

Charges may also be obtained against stock or unit trust securities.

Obtaining a charging order is a two stage process.

- The first stage is an **interim order**.
  - Apply to court
  - may be without notice
  - considered without a hearing; if the interim order is made the judge fixes a date for the second stage hearing
  - the interim order is served on the judgement debtor, on any other creditors as the court directs such as a mortgagee and on any co-owners not less than 21 days before the second stage hearing. A certificate of service is needed if the interim order is served by the judgment creditor and not by the court.
  - remember to register the interim order on the charges register of registered property(or at the central land charges registry should the property still be unregistered title)
  - any written objections to a final charging order are to be filed not less than 7 days before the second stage hearing

- The second stage is the **hearing** to consider whether a final order should be made. The court may
    - discharge the interim order
    - decide/direct a trial on any issues
    - make a final charging order. If made, remember to register the final order on the charges register of a registered property (or at the central land charges registry should the property still be unregistered title) if the interim one was not so registered.

There will be no payment of the debt until the property is sold; or if money is needed now the judgment creditor can bring a Part 8 claim to claim an order for sale if the judgment debtor is sole owner. If the property is co-owned an order for sale would be pursuant to the Trusts of Land and Appointment of Trustees Act 2002.

Third-Party Debt Order

This is an order obtained from the court on application by the judgment creditor, ordering a third party to pay directly to the judgment creditor the amount owed by the judgment debtor.

The third party could be for example the debtor's bank, or her tenant, because
- her bank owes the money in her account to her (the account must be in her sole name if a third party debt order is applied for)
- tenants may owe money to her as a landlord
- people to whom she has provided services may yet be to pay her

Obtaining a third party debt order is a two stage process.

- The first stage is an **interim order**.
    - Apply to court
    - may be without notice
    - considered without a hearing; if the interim order is made the judge fixes a date for the second stage hearing, directing that the third party cannot make any payment which would reduce the amount s/he owes to the judgement debtor to less than the amount specified in the order
    - the interim order is served on the third party not less than 21 days before the second stage hearing. The third party must now freeze anything s/he owes to the judgment debtor
    - the interim order is served on the judgement debtor not less than 7 days after the copy order was served on the third party and not less than 7 days before the second stage hearing. A certificate of service is needed if the interim order is served by the judgment creditor and not by the court.
    - any written objections to a final third party debt order are to be filed not less than 3 days before the second stage hearing

- The second stage is the **hearing** to consider whether a final order should be made. This will be not less than 28 days after the interim order was made. The court may
    - discharge the interim order
    - decide/direct a trial on any issues
    - make a final third party debt order, ordering the third party to pay money to the judgment creditor. The equivalent amount is thus expunged from the third party's debt to the judgment debtor.

Attachment of earnings order

Earnings include fees, wages, bonus and commission, salary, pension and statutory sick pay. The judgment debtor's employer may be ordered to deduct amounts from her pay and pay them to the court.

Where the judgement debtor is employed and has missed one instalment following the judgement and there are no other available assets the judgment creditor can

- make a request to the court.
- The court sends to the judgement debtor a questionnaire in advance of a hearing
- The judgement debtor completes the questionnaire which is considered in the absence of the parties by a court administration officer
- If an order is made it is served on the parties
- If the court officer does not make an order or if there are any objections the matter will go before the District Judge.

ENFORCEMENT OF OTHER JUDGMENTS

- Where the judgment was for the **delivery of goods**
  - **Warrant** of specific delivery in the **County** Court; or
  - **Writ** of specific delivery in the **High** Court
    - Only the goods specified in the judgment can be seized

  - **Warrant** of delivery in the **County** Court; or
  - **Writ** of delivery in the **High** Court
    - Either the goods specified in the judgment can be seized, or other goods to the same value

The claimant makes a request to the court with a draft warrant or writ of (specific) delivery and pays the fee.

At least 7 clear days' notice in prescribed form is given by the enforcement agent/officer to the defendant at her home or business address.

- Where the judgment was for the **possession of land**

  - CPR 83.26 for the County court
    - An application for a warrant of possession may be made without notice to the County Court hearing centre where the judgment or order which it is sought to enforce was made or to which the proceedings have since been transferred.
    - When a debtor wishes to oppose an application for a warrant of possession, transfer it to the County Court hearing centre serving the address where the debtor resides or carries on business, or to another court.
    - The person applying for a warrant of possession must file a certificate that the land which is subject of the judgment or order has not been vacated
    - If D re-enters the property, second time removal is by getting court permission for a warrant of restitution.

  - CPR 83.13 for the High Court
    - Writ against trespassers
    - Court permission needed otherwise for writ
    - Force may be used
    - If D re-enters the property, second time removal is by getting court permission for a writ of restitution.

- Where an **injunction** has been breached, remember that breach amounts to contempt of court. When the court is satisfied beyond reasonable doubt, enforcement is by
  - Up to 2 years imprisonment where the order contained a penal notice
  - Sequestration of assets
  - Other lesser punishments.

Chapter 29 MOCS

For **money** judgments, the method or combination of methods of enforcement will depend on the circumstances of both the judgement debtor and the judgement creditor

For **non**-money judgments, the method of enforcement will depend on the type of judgement

- Delivery of goods
- Land possession
- Injunction breach

Chapter 30

u) JUDICIAL REVIEW

[BSB 25; CPR Parts 8 and 54]

Judicial review is a review of how a public **function** or duty was performed (or not) or decided (or not) by that **public authority**. Public authorities also include inferior courts and tribunals, (though not County Courts, whose decisions should be appealed rather than judicially reviewed. Please see the next chapter on Appeals).

It may be prudent to consider the availability of other remedies before considering judicial review. This is because **court permission** is required to apply for a judicial review. If permission is granted, there will be a **substantive hearing**.

BSB 25.1 The requirements and principles for obtaining permission to claim judicial review

In considering whether it will give permission the court will look at

- The grounds for judicial review, which relate to the lawfulness of an enactment, decision, action or incorrect procedure in the exercise of a public authority's function or duty;
- Whether C has a sufficient interest (i.e. will he be directly affected by the court's decision; is it *his* rights that the public authority has infringed?)
- Whether the papers show an **arguable case on the legal merits**.

BSB 25.2 The availability of remedies of quashing order, mandatory order, prohibiting order, injunction and declaration in judicial review claims.

Remedies available for successful JR claims

- **Prohibitory order**
  This is an order restraining the lower authority from acting outside its jurisdiction.

- **Quashing order**
  This is an order to quash the original decision of the public body. It is available when a decision is so unreasonable that no reasonable person or body properly directing itself to the law would ever make it. (This is known as <u>Wednesbury</u> unreasonableness).

  When the previous decision was made in court or tribunal, in addition to quashing, the High Court can also substitute its own decision where the lower decision was quashed for an error of law without which there could only have been one original decision.

  When the previous decision was made in a court, tribunal or by any other public authority, in addition to quashing, the High Court can also remit the matter, directing that the lower authority reaches a decision in accordance with the findings of the High Court .

- **Mandatory order**
  This is an order requiring the lower authority to fulfil its duties.

- **An injunction**

- **Any of the above and** a declaration, injunction or money award. For a money award the court must be satisfied that C would have won damages in private law.

- **Declaration**
  Where the parties have a real interest in resolving a real question of law or rights the court may exercise its discretion to make a declaration on that point of law or rights.

The JR procedure (CPR Part 8 modified by CPR Part 54)

- There is a pre-action protocol for judicial review in Part C of the White Book
  - letter before claim with copies to all interested parties
  - date and details of the decision being challenged
  - clear summary of facts that the claim is based on
  - D should respond within 14 days to all interested parties

- C issues a JR CF in the Administrative Court office of QBD (note that JR for planning matters is in the Planning Court). The CF must be issued **promptly within 3 months** of the grounds of that claim arising. The court may grant an extension of that 3 months (unlikely unless the court considers that
  - there is good reason for extending the time limit or
  - there is adequate explanation for the delay and
  - extending the time limit will not cause substantial hardship or substantial prejudice or be detrimental to good administration)

- The CF to bring a JR claim needs to state
  - the issues raised
  - which enactment the claim is regarding, if any
  - the name and address of those C considers an interested party (i.e. those directly affected by the claim)
  - any (interim) remedies claimed
  - that it asks for court permission to bring the JR claim

- C serves CF **within 7 days of issue** on D and on interested parties named in the CF unless the court orders otherwise

- AOS filed **by 21 days after CF** deemed receipt

- AOS served on C and interested parties **at the latest 7 days after filing** but as soon as practicable. (AOS defaulter may not take part in hearing to decide whether permission is given to proceed unless the court directs otherwise)

- The permission 'hearing' is usually a paper exercise only.
  - If refused because the application is considered without merit, C cannot ask for a subsequent oral hearing to consider permission again
  - Otherwise following a paper refusal, C can request an oral hearing **within 7 days after service of the reasons for refusal**. The court gives parties and any AOS server at least 2 days' notice of the hearing date, unless the court orders otherwise
  - D / other interested parties need not attend this reconsideration hearing.
  - If permission is refused at the oral hearing, C can apply for permission to appeal to the Court of Appeal.

- Once permission is granted, the court can direct either a stay or that the substantive hearing date be set. Neither D nor any other person served with the CF may apply to set aside an order giving permission to proceed.

- An AOS defaulter can file and serve a response and any written evidence within 35 days of service of an order granting JR permission and can then take part in any JR hearing

- C must file and serve a skeleton argument not less than 21 working days before the hearing date; other parties not less than 14 working days.

- Note that usually
  - the hearing is in public (unless it needs to be in private, pursuant to the general rule in CPR 39.2(3))
  - no disclosure is required unless the court expressly orders it; it is also possible to make an interim application for disclosure or for other interim orders – further information, injunction or permission to XX.
  - no oral evidence is given. Written evidence must be served as per part 54 CPR.

Chapter 30 MOCS

JR is a review of public body decisions.

Court permission is needed to bring a JR claim.

Note the procedure, including the pre-action protocol and the 6 possible remedies.

Chapter 31

v) APPEALS

[BSB 26; CPR Part 52]

The sessions dealing with this area of the syllabus on my BPTC course are	

BSB 26.1 **The principles and procedures governing civil appeals in England and Wales (excluding appeals to the Supreme Court), comprising permission to routes of appeal, time for appealing, appellant's notice and grounds on which an appeal may succeed, fresh evidence in appeals, respondent's notice, and skeleton arguments.**

A decision made in a lower court can be appealed to a higher, appellate court.

Appeal courts can affirm / set aside / vary what happened in the lower court, or order a new trial. *affirm/vary/order set aside/new trial*

Unless the court orders otherwise, bringing an appeal does not stay the decision of the lower court and the decision can be enforced. Therefore **A should apply for a stay of the proceedings in the lower court when applying for permission to appeal.** *↳ unless court orders otherwise!*

BSB 26 **Routes of appeal and permission to appeal**

The Table 1 appeal destination table in the White book may be depicted as follows:-

Part 7 other than multi track; Part 7 SJ/strike out including multi-track; Part 8 claims		
From the lower court		**To the higher (appellate) court**

District judge in the County Court	**Need permission**
	Unless
	
	• person in contempt of court wants to appeal an immediate or suspended prison sentence
	• appealing against
	   o refusal to grant habeas corpus
	   o a Children Act secure accommodation order
	
	Permission from either the lower court orally at the end of the hearing in the lower court after costs have been awarded **or** by applying to the appellate court. The test is RPOS or SOCR. **(BSB 26 grounds on which an appeal may succeed)**
		Circuit judge in County Court

Circuit judge in the County Court		High Court judge
Master or district judge in the High Court		High Court judge
High Court judge		Court of Appeal

Real prospect of success OR some other compelling reason

145

Or put another way, the Table 1 appeal destination table in the White book may also be depicted as follows (where (P) = permission to appeal is required, unless one of the exceptions in the box above applies)

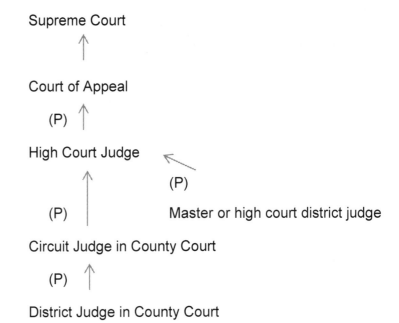

Assignment of appeals to the Court of Appeal – (leap-frogging)

As regards those appeals circled in the diagram below, the courts can, either as the lower court or as the higher court, where it considers that appeals would make an important point of principle or practice or if there is some other compelling reason for the Court of Appeal to hear it, order a transfer to the Court of Appeal or the Master of Rolls can so direct. The Court of Appeal or the Master of the Rolls may also remit it back!

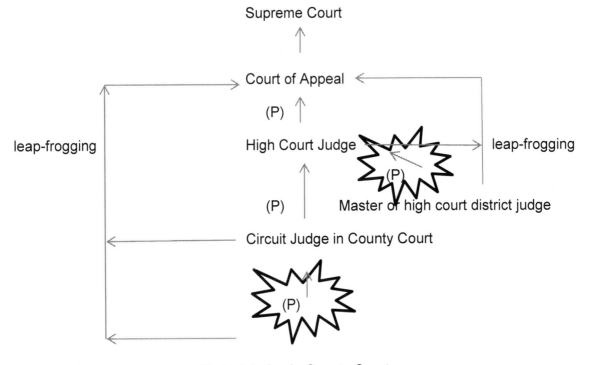

Part 7 multi-track final decision of the entire proceedings
(i.e. it would be if it were not an appeal or if there were no detailed assessment of costs)
or specialist company proceedings

From the lower court		To the higher (appellate) court

Circuit judge in the County Court	**As above,**
	need permission
	Unless
	• person in contempt of court wants to appeal an immediate or suspended prison sentence
	• appealing against
	    ○ refusal to grant habeas corpus
	    ○ a Children Act secure accommodation order
	
	Permission from either the lower court orally at the end of the hearing in the lower court after costs have been awarded **or** by applying to the appellate court. The test is RPOS or SOCR. **(BSB 26 grounds on which an appeal may succeed)**
		Court of Appeal

Master or High Court District Judge		Court of Appeal
High Court judge		Court of Appeal

Or put another way (where (P) = permission to appeal is required, unless one of the exceptions in the box above applies)

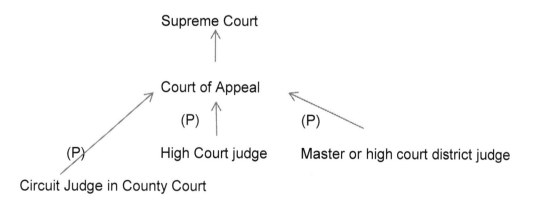

Second Appeals		
From the lower court	→	**To the higher (appellate) court**
Circuit judge in County Court	As above, need permission unless person in contempt of court wants to appeal on immediate or suspended prison sentence. Permission is **only from the Court of Appeal on the grounds that there is** • an important point of principle or practice; or • SOCR for CA to hear it. **(BSB 26 grounds on which an appeal may succeed**	Court of Appeal
Master or High Court District Judge		Court of Appeal
High Court judge		Court of Appeal
Court of Appeal	→	Supreme Court

Overview of the procedure for making an appeal

Where permission to appeal is not required the Appellant notifies the Respondent.

Where permission to appeal is required, please refer to the flow chart on the next page. This includes **BSB 26** **Time for appealing, appellant's notice, and respondent's notice.**

Details of the contents of the Appellant's notice ("AN"), any respondent's notice ("RN") and the appeal bundle are on the page after that.

LC ruling – may apply [test is **RPOS** or **SOCR**] orally at end of hearing **or** to AC within 21 days of LC decision / within time frame directed by LC

Note - For second appeals must be within 21 days, and the AC is CA

Grounds to be identified: important principle/practice or SOCR

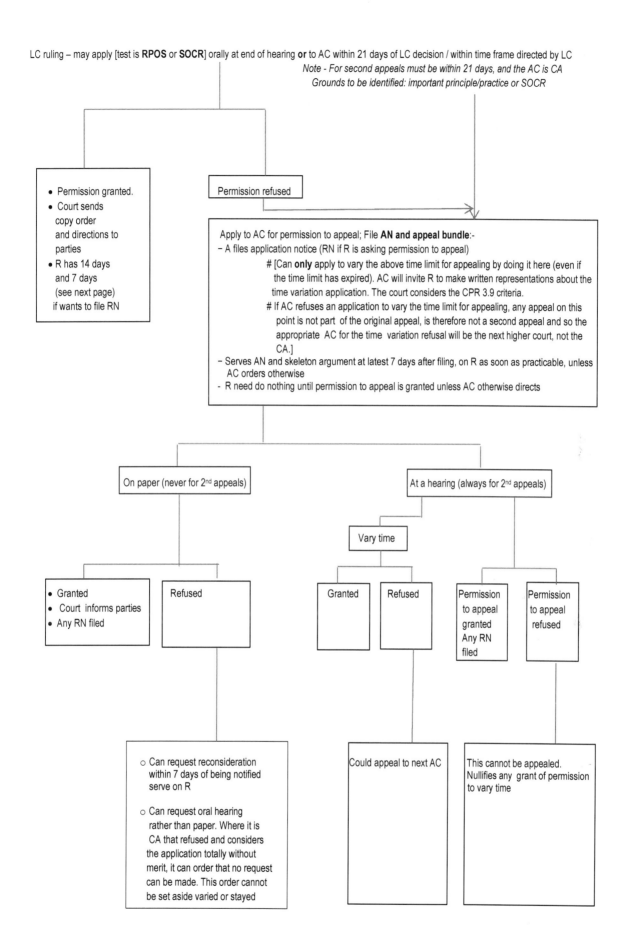

- Permission granted.
- Court sends
  copy order
  and directions to
  parties
- R has 14 days
  and 7 days
  (see next page)
  if wants to file RN

Permission refused

Apply to AC for permission to appeal; File **AN and appeal bundle**:-
– A files application notice (RN if R is asking permission to appeal)
  # [Can **only** apply to vary the above time limit for appealing by doing it here (even if
    the time limit has expired). AC will invite R to make written representations about the
    time variation application. The court considers the CPR 3.9 criteria.
  # If AC refuses an application to vary the time limit for appealing, any appeal on this
    point is not part of the original appeal, is therefore not a second appeal and so the
    appropriate AC for the time variation refusal will be the next higher court, not the
    CA.]
– Serves AN and skeleton argument at latest 7 days after filing, on R as soon as practicable, unless
  AC orders otherwise
- R need do nothing until permission to appeal is granted unless AC otherwise directs

On paper (never for 2nd appeals)

At a hearing (always for 2nd appeals)

Vary time

- Granted
- Court informs parties
- Any RN filed

Refused

Granted

Refused

Permission
to appeal
granted
Any RN
filed

Permission
to appeal
refused

o Can request reconsideration
  within 7 days of being notified
  serve on R

o Can request oral hearing
  rather than paper. Where it is
  CA that refused and considers
  the application totally without
  merit, it can order that no request
  can be made. This order cannot
  be set aside varied or stayed

Could appeal to next AC

This cannot be appealed.
Nullifies any grant of permission
to vary time

Contents of the **Appellant's Appeal Notice** applying for permission to appeal

The notice is on form **N161**, to set out
- why the LC was wrong; whether the appeal is on an error of fact/law; A needs to show that no reasonable judge using discretion could have reached the same decision
- may include an application to vary the time limit for appealing (i.e. if out of time for this)
- may include application for interim remedies

A needs AC permission if A subsequently wishes to amend the AN.

Contents of the appeal bundle for filing and serving include:

- sealed copy Appellant's notice including copy LC judgement transcript
- sealed copy of the order being appealed
- skeleton argument of A's Counsel [may be filed after the rest of the bundle, but within 14 days of the filing of the AN] (cost sanctions if don't); PDs to Part 52 set out the required contents of skeleton arguments. In addition please cross refer to your advocacy training
- relevant statements of case
- other matters that A considers reasonably necessary as set out in the PDs to Part 52.

Following service on R, as per the diagram on the previous page, there will be either a paper exercise or a hearing to either grant or refuse permission to appeal.

Where the AC grants permission to appeal

- Respondents Notice
  - If the Respondent wishes to ask the appeal court to uphold or vary the order of the lower court for reasons different from or additional to those given by the lower court, the Respondent must file an appeal notice **(Respondent's Notice, form N162)** setting out those different/additional reasons or the grounds for variation. (This notice is not needed if the Respondent wishes the decision to be upheld for the same reasons as in lower court).
  - The Respondent must file any respondent's notice within 14 days after the appellant's notice was served on her
  - The Respondent must serve it as soon as practicable, at the latest 7 days after filing it, on the Appellant and on any other Respondent.

- A must add the following documents to the appeal bundle for the appeal itself
  - R's notice and skeleton argument (if any)
  - the parts of transcript evidence directly relevant to the question at issue on the appeal
  - the order granting permission to appeal (or the transcript or note of the judgement where it was giving at oral hearing)
  - any documents that A and R have agreed to add as a result of amendments agreed between A and R.

Where permission to appeal is refused on a particular issue A must remove documents relevant only to that issue from the bundle.

At the appeal hearing

- Unless the court considers it would be in the interests of justice to hold a re-hearing, it reviews the LC decision.
- **BSB 26   Fresh evidence in appeals.** There is no oral evidence and no evidence that was not before LC unless the court orders otherwise.

Applications to adduce fresh evidence need to be in a separate bundle.

AC may admit fresh evidence (rare) if AC thinks it's in the interests of justice to actually rehear; this discretion is exercised by consideration of the Ladd v Marshall principles (and the overriding objective). The principles are
- reasonable diligence could not have obtained the evidence for use at LC trial; and
- the evidence would probably have an important influence on the result; and
- the evidence was apparently credible

– AC has the power to
- affirm, set aside or vary any order or judgment made or given by the lower court;
- refer any claim or issue for determination by the lower court;
- order a new trial or hearing;
- make orders for the payment of interest;
- make a costs order. (Where a Part 36 offer was made in the main proceedings, a new offer needs to be made where a party wants Part 36 protection in relation to the appeal)

Chapter 31 NO MOCS!

APPENDIX ONE

Suggested ways to use this book

There is no point diving into Civil Litigation, Evidence and Remedies at the deep end. The primary aim of this book is to help you understand the process so that you can more easily retain it for assessment purposes and for the rest of your career. It is strongly recommended that you become familiar with the contents of the appendices of this book before starting work on the civil litigation process itself.

It is hoped that this book will provide a useful interactive revision guide for those who first come to it at the beginning of their final revision process.

It is further hoped that those students who wish to get ahead with understanding the process of civil litigation before starting the BPTC course will find this book to be a helpful framework on which to base their studies. It is intended to be accessible to the civil litigation novice who needs to be ready for assessment in civil litigation and pupillage in the course of just one academic year.

This book follows the progress of a claim in the civil courts from pre-action through to trial and beyond, dealing with every element of the syllabus for the BPTC assessment as set by the Bar Standards Board. This may not necessarily be the order in which the required content for the centrally set assessment in Civil Litigation, Evidence and Remedies is set out on the website of the Bar Standards Board, nor the order in which your BPTC course provider teaches the syllabus. For this reason you are invited to fill in the cross referencing boxes at the beginning of each chapter of this book with the session number allocated to the topic when it is taught by your course provider.

Please note that in the flowchart setting out the progress of a claim, matters are mentioned at the very first point in time that it is possible for them occur in real life. Please also be aware that there are many considerations to be dealt with before a matter is first brought to the court's attention, so do not be disappointed when this book does not use issuing documents at court as its starting point!

This book uses abbreviated note form and diagrams wherever possible to aid understanding and learning. It is best used either as pre-reading for the BPTC, as pre-reading to get an overview of the topic before you encounter it on your BPTC, or as revision following completion of the course. It is a supplement to the BPTC. It is **NOT** a replacement for it nor is it a quick fix substitution for student engagement with the course. It is therefore imperative that you flesh out the note form and diagrammatic contents of this book with the teaching by your BPTC Provider and by reference to the White Book.

That said, you are strongly recommended and encouraged to engage with the activities in this book as a supplement to your BPTC so that your learning will be deep learning. In this way your knowledge should be retained for long periods of time, as contrasted with superficial learning where you would soon forget much of the material. In this way it is anticipated that you will not find yourself in the position where you need to learn and revise the whole course as the final assessment approaches; rather you will have understood, practised and retained it in an incremental manner as you progressed through the course or through your revision.

Compare study on the BPTC to learning a musical instrument to grade 8 standard. You would probably have to practise your instrument for several hours a day over many years to achieve that standard. A person could not expect to cram that many hours of practice into the days or weeks immediately preceding their grade 8 music assessment. It is the same with learning the knowledge and skills required for lawyering.

There is no substitute for becoming conversant with the White Book itself.

In the MOCS at the end of chapters many of the rules or tenets have been distilled down to an absolute minimum. You are warned that this absolute minimum may mean nothing to you unless and until you have read / noted / learned / understood / remembered / mastered the art of applying the relevant civil procedure rules and with them any associated teaching from your BPTC provider.

APPENDIX TWO

The White Book.

When a party wishes to make a civil claim against another party, the procedure to be followed in England and Wales is set out in the White Book. This is the colloquial term for the volumes called Civil Procedure, published by Sweet and Maxwell. It is very likely that your Provider will furnish you with a copy of this for your BPTC.

The White Book is made up of 2 volumes and both volumes are renewed each year. During the course of any one year cumulative supplements are produced, updating the rules as the year progresses. We must all therefore ensure that we are following the current rules by using the White Book printed for the current year together with any cumulative supplements to date.

The principal volume for the BPTC will be Volume 1 which sets out in section A the civil procedure rules (usually abbreviated to CPR). In turn, these rules in section A are divided into 86 parts. You will therefore hear reference to "Part 1 of the CPR" which sets out the overriding objective or "Part 23" when dealing with general rules about applications for court orders.

Once you have access to the White Book, take a look at 1.1, 1.2 and 1.3. You will see that these are the first three rules of the CPR in Part 1, dealing with the overriding objective and that the **CPR rules** themselves are printed in **bold type**.

Before we reach CPR 1.4, there is lots of very small type. This is commentary on the rules and not the rules themselves. Your provider will indicate to you which parts of the commentary you should read in detail. The commentary is just that: a commentary, setting out comments on the way that each of the CPR rules has been applied. You will use the commentary much more frequently when you are actually out in practice.

Next please turn to Part 2 of the CPR, "Application and interpretation of the rules". At the end of the section of this Part, as with all other Parts, you will find a series of pages beginning with the title, "Practice Direction". These practice directions are important and give directions as to how the rule operates in practice. You will need to know the contents of these **practice directions** as well as the CPR rules for your assessment and beyond.

The first practice direction in Part 2 is called "Practice Direction 2A-court offices". You will see that on the right-hand side of the page in bold are the numbered practice directions for this section. Although these are now set out to read, for example 2APD.1, you may often hear them referred to as practice direction 2A, paragraph or note 1. Do not let this confuse you; it is two ways of saying exactly the same thing.

Continuing on through practice direction A Part 2, you will see that there is also a section 2B containing the various elements making up PD 2B (2BPD.1 etc.).

You are not expected to learn the individual numbering of the elements of the CPR for your assessment although you are expected to know their content. For this reason and because from year-to-year it is not unheard of for the numbering of paragraphs in each part of the CPR to change, even if only slightly, then, unless I feel that it is helpful for explanatory purposes in this book, I will not be referring to the internal numbering of each Part, but only to each Part in its entirety in the heading of each chapter.

Another very useful section of the White Book is that which begins by listing the pre-action conduct and protocols before setting out the detail of them. When you hear your tutor refer to, for example, "the pre-action protocols", or to choose one, such as the "pre-action protocol for personal injury claims", you may find it useful to know that they are set out in section C of the White Book and you need not look anywhere else for them.

Section D of Volume one of the White Book is a section often overlooked by students until they are pointed in its direction. This is a useful section for summarising the CPR and you may find it helpful to refer to that in addition to your consideration of the rules themselves in section A.

Most importantly, there can be no substitute for getting to know your way around the White Book and getting to grips with its content. Please do not defer referring to it. Start to become conversant with it from day one.

I appreciate that the White Book is heavy to carry about on a daily basis, together with all the other materials for your course. You can access the Civil Procedure rules in electronic form from the UK government website www.justice.gov.uk by clicking on 'procedure rules' under the heading 'most popular' at the top of the homepage. This will not give you the commentary from the White Book but it is a useful source of the rules themselves.

APPENDIX THREE

Some study ideas

We all have different strengths and weaknesses, we all have our preferred ways of studying. You have all been successful in completing your education up to the end of the academic stage of legal training, otherwise you would not be studying on the BPTC.

This section of the book sets out suggestions of possible new ways to study a subject about which you will need to retain knowledge for life, not only for the current academic year.

Some of them you may already be using, some of them may seem a little bit off the wall. Some of them may feel like common sense to you, some may appear so obvious that you will be surprised that you have never thought of them before. Some of them have been around as learning tools not only for centuries but maybe for millennia. Feel free to pick and choose between them to find the best method of learning for you.

I have seen many students who approach the course by trying to learn its content by rote and by this I mean simply writing it out again and again and again in the hope that it will eventually stick. Perhaps by considering some of the suggestions in this appendix, studying could become less of a chore (!).

I will start with the best piece of advice I think that I can give you, whatever your preferred learning style. Whenever you need something clarifying from this book / BPTC large group sessions / BPTC small group sessions / your own notes, the best solution is to go to the original source of the CPR in the White Book. With a little time and thought, you will find it clearer and much less daunting than you may at first sight have thought.

Purely as a learning aid, you will note that in this book I have sometimes moved away from the classic jargon of the CPR; for example rather than use a term such as "unsuccessful party" or "successful party" I will use instead the terms "loser" and "winner". By doing this it is hoped that you may find it easier to understand what is happening before re-imposing the original CPR wording into your learning.

Next, please be warned that assessment in civil litigation, evidence and remedies on the BPTC will not necessarily be fully confined to what you have learned in your "civil litigation" module. The whole process of civil litigation as taught on the BPTC encompasses not only the knowledge you will gain from the civil litigation module itself, but also from the further knowledge and skills you will assimilate from your studies in opinion writing, drafting and advocacy. It is vital that you enter the civil litigation and evidence and remedies assessment room prepared to use all of those knowledge and skills in the round. They supplement and complement each other; the days of learning individual modules in a discrete box are now gone for you.

I would suggest that you try to be disciplined in the way that you approach the course as the weeks go by. Those things that you have no choice but to "learn by heart", you will find easy to do if you do them piecemeal weekly rather than saving them up for a final grand learning session immediately before the assessment.

The assessments for both civil litigation and criminal litigation are currently set two days apart. If you are starting the BPTC full-time you need to ensure that you are fully aware of how to keep the two processes totally separate in your mind. (Those studying the BPTC part-time may be lucky enough to have those assessments in 2 separate years).

One way to do this could be to colour code your notes. You could use different coloured paper/backgrounds, one for civil and one for criminal: you could use different styles of font and/or different colours of font when typing up your notes for each, or different coloured pens when writing up your notes.

There now follow two methods of committing lists to memory. I have already mentioned that some students' method is to simply repeat writing out the lists. The methods I'm about to share may initially take a little time to master and establish, but you may find them more effective in the long run.

Linking

The first method is a method which links items in a list. Please turn to the chapter in this book called INTERIM INJUNCTIONS ("II"). It contains a list, required by the Bar Standards Board syllabus at point 18.3 - **BSB 18.3** **The principles governing the exceptions and variations to American Cyanamid.**

It matters not, that if you are reading this book before you have studied the BPTC, that you as yet have no idea what American Cyanamid is, let alone the exceptions and variations to it! I am simply using this as a demonstration of one method for list learning and if you subscribe to it and choose to use it, (even better if you devise your own linking method for the same list) it may be that you will still be able to recite the list of exceptions and variations by the time you reach American Cyanamid on your course.

The key is to start by visualising the first item in the list in a very vivid way, attaching an emotion to it. The more weird, crazy and wonderful you make it the more likely it is to be easily retrievable when you need it.

The first item on the list is "a mandatory interim injunction". Since the chapter in the book is called interim injunctions, I am taking it that you will not need any help in remembering those two words. So the first item on the list is "mandatory".

For this I will visualise a girl I know call Amanda (she is of course American, so that her name is pronounced "Ay-manda" (a manda)) and dress her in the blue colour of the Tory party. ("Ay-manda-Tory (a mandatory)). The Tory colour blue is so right that it hurts my eyes and I have to shield them to stop my eyes hurting.

Next on the list are interim injunctions that "finally dispose of the case".

The American Amanda in her blue Tory clothes that hurt my eyes is carrying a case. This case is really tiny and keeps getting caught in her fingers. She has been trying to dispose of it by shaking her fingers but it has remained stuck. Finally she manages to dispose of it and is so happy that she lets out a deafening whoop of joy. She has finally disposed of the case.

Next on the list are cases where there is "no arguable defence".

When she shook off the case, it flew into *the* fence and hit a sign pinned to it which said in letters dripping with blood, which made me shiver, "Do not argue with the bull". ("No argue – a bull" (no arguable) and "*the* fence" sounds like defence). The bull has blood around its mouth and on the ring through its nose. It starts to charge towards me and I feel scared.

Next on the list are "restraint of trade" cases.

I need to restrain the bull, but I can't because it charges past me onto a train and I feel huge relief. It is a steam train and the steam is forming the word TRADE in the sky which floats towards me and makes me have a coughing fit.

<u>Defamation claims</u>.

The coughing fit lasts for 3 years and my rib cage is very painful as a result. Another result is that I find **fame** and that **fame** leads to people saying terrible things about me. This makes me cry.

<u>Freedom of expression</u>

"Cry Freedom" is the title of the autobiography of Nelson Mandela where he expresses itself very well and I am happy to read it and learn from it.

<u>Privacy</u>

I happily go to read it in the toilet, which has a pleasant smell of air freshener. This is the best place to get privacy, which is why an old-fashioned word for toilet is "privvy".

If you have been happy to actively engage with this, at first, seemingly convoluted way of committing something to memory, perhaps you could try recalling the list, say 3 days after you first did this exercise. You should be surprised at how easily you retrieve the list without any hard grind of repetitive writing or constant recitations from memory. You could further test it out by having one of your colleagues who does not use this linking method, learning the list at the same time as you. Insist that you both pledge not to look at it again for 3 days and then see who has the easier recall in 3 days' time.

If you refresh your weird and wonderful linking story in your mind for a few seconds twice a week, that should be enough for you to constantly be able to retrieve it without straining your memory.

<u>Locus</u>

I have chosen to call this second method "Locus" in the subheading as the phrase "Locus Standi" should be familiar to students of law.

Locus is the Latin word for "place"; this second method for recording lists where getting the order right is important is known as the "Loci" (places) method.

Here you settle on a list of places that you know well; so well, that recalling them instantly in the same order every time will not be a problem or an effort for you. You may choose a room in a building that you know well, like your childhood home and within that home use rooms whose layout has remained constant. Or you may choose a route that you know well. I use the route on my way home from the train station, followed by my garden and then the rooms in my house.

Again, using any list you wish to learn, you attach these weird, unusual, emotion provoking images to each of your Loci. Since your Loci will always come in the same order, this should prevent you from forgetting which one comes next.

Please turn to chapter 25 in this book. **BSB 27** requires you to know the form of experts' reports.

I will share with you the first few of these attached to my personal Loci; you may then choose to learn this list with your own Loci. Do remember to refresh your mental images a couple of times a week.

The first 4 of my Loci are: –

- the railway sign at the train station
- the parish noticeboard on the corner

- the post box
- the street sign of the road where I live

1. <u>Expert reports must be addressed to the court</u>
   I visualise a dress and a pair of court shoes attached to the railway sign. They are flapping in the wind and making a huge noise and I'm frustrated because I cannot jump up to reach them.

2. <u>Expert reports must set out the expert's qualifications and experience</u>
   The parish noticeboard is covered with so many diplomas and certificates that there is no room for anything else. They are pinned to the board several on top of each other and people are gathering round commenting to each other how very, very clever this particular expert must be.

3. <u>Expert reports must give details of literature relied on in making the report</u>
   JK Rowling is at the post box posting copies of all the books that I studied for English literature at school. The books are so detailed that they make a large thudding sound as each one goes in to the box.

4. <u>Expert reports must set out the substance of the facts and instructions material to the opinions of the expert</u>
   The street sign is smeared with a glue-like substance which has a powerful smell, but it has to be powerful to attach the pieces of cloth and material to it which the council are now using to decorate all street signs.

Of course if you have used the Loci of your journey home from the rail station to remember the contents of an expert's report, then you will not want to use it for other lists! You could therefore consider allocating your garden to one area of procedure, your kitchen to another and your bedroom to another. A quick mental recap every few days may alleviate and lessen the tension of having lots to commit to memory at a later stage in the course.

| Further study ideas and suggestions |

- You may be the kind of person who would benefit from grouping matters of the same kind together as you progress through the course/this book, as an aide memoir for revision later on.

   When coming to grips with the CPR you will notice that

   - there are some things that a court or a party will or <u>must</u> do; there are some things that a court or a party <u>may</u> do;
   - there are some things that you need the court's permission to do;
   - there are some things that are a rule "unless court orders otherwise";
   - there are some elements of rules where each and every one of them needs to be fulfilled;
   - there are some elements of rules where only one of the matters in the alternative needs to be fulfilled - do you need A **AND** B **AND** C **AND** D before you can make an application to court; or do you need just one of A **OR** B **OR** C **OR** D?

   If it works for you, you could create separate revision pages for each of the above.

- Those students who have formed small study groups seem to improve their learning and understanding more quickly and easily than those who choose to always study alone.

There are things you can do on your own to enhance your learning; there are even more you can do when working in a committed way with a few of your colleagues.

- For example, you could agree that within the next 24 hours you would each learn, in your preferred way, a list from what you studied on the course last week. Then over lunch you could randomly ask a colleague to recite it, perhaps timing each other and forming a league table amongst yourselves as to the quickest/slowest/most accurate!

- Some students like to use flashcards and you could devise innovative ways of using these to test and help each other.

- Your provider will give you practice in answering in MCQ's and SAQ's throughout the course.

  Another lunchtime 'game' could be way you reprise the MCQ's/SAQ's that you recently have answered on your course. Keep asking each other the same questions so that you meet them more than several times, quite frequently. This is another way to keep the knowledge fresh in your mind's so that you are not trying to learn volumes in the period immediately before the assessment.

  You will become conversant with the way that MCQ's are posed and I would strongly recommend that you use small study groups to help each other ensure that you fully understand how and why the correct answers are reached.

- As for answering SAQs, it really is the oldest, most obvious advice that is the best: Answer the questions! It really can be as simple as distilling the questions asked in, say, a question worth 3 marks, to each of its component parts.

Some students have told me that they make a subheading for themselves of each of these component parts and leave a few lines blank before writing down the second subheading and a further few blank lines before writing down the third subheading and so on. That way they expect not miss out answering any one element of the question.

For each of the subheadings they jot down a distillation of the main points/lists in relation to that area of law. They then apply the facts of the scenario to each of those points; some of them may be relevant, some of them may not be relevant. This could be a way of making sure that students address their mind to all the possible points that the scenario is concerned with. Once they have eliminated those that are not relevant to the fact pattern they feel they can apply the relevant law to the relevant facts and actually answer the question.

Whether you use any of the study tips above or prefer to stick to those that you have tried and tested in your assessments so far, I wish you the very best both for your time on the BPTC and in your careers beyond.

APPENDIX FOUR

Required content for the centrally set assessment in

Civil Litigation, Evidence and Remedies

for the BPTC as set by the Bar Standards Board

You can access a copy in the BPTC Handbook on the BSB website

(sub-section numbers have been added for ease of reference in this book)

BSB		Chapter
1.	**Organisational matters**	
1.1	the organisation of the High Court (in outline);	1
1.2	the organisation of the County Courts (in outline);	1
1.3	the allocation of business between the High and County Courts (in outline);	1
1.4	the allocation of business between tracks;	1
1.5	the overriding objective of the Civil Procedure Rules; and	1
1.6	the impact of the Human Rights Act on civil claims.	1
2.	**Pre-action conduct and pre-action protocols**	
2.1	the Practice Direction (Pre-Action Conduct);	10
2.2	the list of specific pre action protocols; the principles relating to pre action conduct under the Personal Injury pre-action protocol;	10
2.3	the details of pre-action conduct where no specific protocol applies; and	10
2.4	the consequences of non-compliance with pre-action protocols.	10
3.	**Limitation**	9
3.1	rules on calculating limitation (accrual and when time stops running);	9
3.2	limitation periods in tort, latent damage cases, personal injuries, fatal accidents, contract, recovery of land, judicial review and contribution claims. Also the provisions of the Limitation Act 1980, ss 14, 14A, 14B and 33; and	9
3.3	Limitation Act 1980 provisions dealing with persons under a disability, fraud, concealment and mistake.	9
4.	**Commencing proceedings**	
4.1	when the Part 7 procedure is appropriate and how Part 7 claims are commenced;	11
4.2	when the Part 8 procedure is appropriate and how Part 8 claims are commenced;	11
4.3	the rules governing service of court documents within the jurisdiction;	11
4.4	the principles governing the validity and renewal of claim forms;	11
4.5	the procedures for bringing and settling proceedings by or against: children and persons suffering from mental incapacity; and	11

162

164

27. Civil Evidence

All the following rules are to be considered in the context of civil claims on the fast track and multi-track.

gwoodworth.upfish.law@gmail.com

All tuition includes one initial orientation session of up to one hour and usually takes place in London at a location of your choice. The orientation session becomes free once you have completed four hours of tuition; i.e. four *x* one-hour sessions, two sessions of two consecutive hours or a mix of these.

For enquiries regarding tuition for areas outside of London, please email me.

All payments must be made in advance of the sessions either in cash on the day or by prior transfer to the relevant Upfish account.

I would like to thank you for buying this book. I hope that it has helped you on your way towards an enjoyable and successful career at the Bar.

Any feedback to help enhance future editions will be gratefully received.

Gillian Woodworth